Synthesis Lectures on Information Concepts, Retrieval, and Services

Series Editor

Gary Marchionini, School of Information and Library Science, The University of North Carolina at Chapel Hill, Chapel Hill, USA

This series publishes short books on topics pertaining to information science and applications of technology to information discovery, production, distribution, and management. Potential topics include: data models, indexing theory and algorithms, classification, information architecture, information economics, privacy and identity, scholarly communication, bibliometrics and webometrics, personal information management, human information behavior, digital libraries, archives and preservation, cultural informatics, information retrieval evaluation, data fusion, relevance feedback, recommendation systems, question answering, natural language processing for retrieval, text summarization, multimedia retrieval, multilingual retrieval, and exploratory search.

Varun Gupta

Libraries as Hubs for Entrepreneurship

Support, AI Experimentation, Practical Technologies, Monitoring, and Evaluation

 Springer

Varun Gupta (ID)
Multidisciplinary Research Centre for
Innovations in SMEs (MrciS)
Gisma University of Applied Sciences
Potsdam, Germany

Department of Economics and Business
Administration
University of Alcala
Alcalá de Henares (Madrid), Spain

ISSN 1947-945X   ISSN 1947-9468   (electronic)
Synthesis Lectures on Information Concepts, Retrieval, and Services
ISBN 978-3-032-03568-4   ISBN 978-3-032-03569-1   (eBook)
https://doi.org/10.1007/978-3-032-03569-1

This Springer imprint is published by the registered company Springer Nature Switzerland AG
The registered company address is: Gewerbestrasse 11, 6330 Cham, Switzerland

If disposing of this product, please recycle the paper.

This book is Dedicated to

My book is dedicated to my parents as well as the almighty Goddesses Koyla, Myah Bhagwati, Jalpa Mata, and Naina Mata.

Mi libro está dedicada a mis padres y a las diosas todopoderosas Koyla, Myah Bhagwati, Jalpa Mata y Naina Mata.

Mein Buch ist sowohl meinen Eltern als auch den allmächtigen Göttinnen Koyla, Myah Bhagwati, Jalpa Mata und Naina Mata gewidmet.

Preface

This book presents the research findings on the role of libraries in supporting entrepreneurship, particularly through the integration of artificial intelligence (AI) and emerging digital technologies. It explores how libraries can enhance their business support services by leveraging AI adoption, co-creation, and structured experimentation while addressing ethical considerations and monitoring and evaluation (M&E) frameworks.

The book includes concrete cases from leading libraries—University of Toronto Libraries, Baker Library at Harvard, and the Public Library of Toronto (Toronto Reference Library, TRL)—as well as from several public libraries funded through the American Library Association's (ALA) Libraries Build Business program initiative, illustrating how libraries are advancing business support services through structured programs and strategic partnerships.

The research examines AI adoption models from both librarians' and entrepreneurs' perspectives, investigates co-creation and experimentation-driven approaches to AI implementation, and proposes a structured AI experimentation policy that balances innovation with ethical considerations. Additionally, it identifies practical AI technologies that libraries can integrate to enhance their business support services. The findings contribute to digital innovation, entrepreneurship, and library science by providing actionable insights for library professionals, entrepreneurs, policymakers, and researchers.

In addition to its scholarly and theoretical depth, this book is grounded in practice. A defining feature of this work is its inclusion of numerous real-world case studies drawn from actual consulting engagements with academic and public libraries. These library cases—spanning institutions of various sizes—offer concrete illustrations of how AI technologies, co-creation, experimentation, and structured monitoring and evaluation (M&E) practices are being implemented in real-world settings. By showcasing these grounded examples, the book provides useful insights that peer libraries can adopt, adapt, or build upon according to their local needs and capacities.

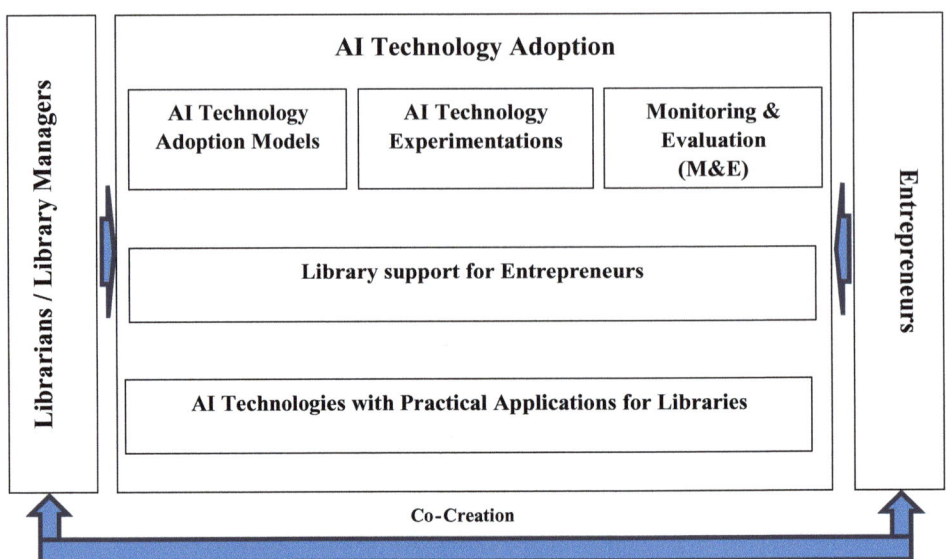

Fig. 1 Research areas addressed by the book

Further, the book includes ready-to-use instructional reference guides for three prac-tical AI tools—ASReview, Connected Papers, and Citation Gecko. These guides are designed to assist libraries in experimenting with or implementing these tools either internally or by offering them directly to patrons. Whether aiming to initiate AI-driven lit-erature reviews or support entrepreneurial research, these guides offer actionable pathways for hands-on application, even in libraries with limited technical expertise. In addition, the book provides practical tools—including business case templates, an AI experimentation policy, and structured AI experimentation reporting forms—which libraries can adopt, adapt, or apply based on their unique contexts and service priorities.

This book disseminates research across six core research areas, graphically outlined in Fig. 1 and explored further in the discussion that follows.

An overview of the six key research areas are provided in Fig. 1. The following sec-tions briefly describe each area as investigated in this book, briefly outlining the themes, contexts, examples, and case studies explored in the respective studies.

- **Library Support for Entrepreneurship**—Examining how libraries function as innova-tion enablers by offering business support services, partnerships, and digital knowledge tools. The study highlights business support services offered by public and aca-demic libraries, including access to bibliographic databases, market research assistance, business incubation programs, digital literacy training, networking opportunities, and collaboration with external innovation actors. Notably, business support services of University of Toronto Libraries, Baker Library at Harvard University, Public Library of Toronto (Toronto Reference Library (TRL)), and some of the public libraries funded under the American Library Association's (ALA) Libraries Build Business Program initiative, are reported. These libraries play a crucial role in supporting entrepreneurs by equipping them with essential resources, industry insights, and technological tools to navigate the complexities of business development and expansion.

- **AI Adoption Factors for Librarians and Entrepreneurs**—Identifying the key drivers and barriers influencing AI adoption in libraries and startup ecosystems. By strengthening these adoption factors, libraries can cultivate a collaborative AI experimentation environment that encourages AI adoption by both librarians and entrepreneurs, while enabling them to co-create experiments. Through continuous experimentation and evaluation, they can make informed decisions collaboratively about adopting or switching AI tools, based on rational assessments of their effectiveness. A case study is also provided that demonstrate how co-experimentation between a mid-sized public library, local entrepreneurs, and the author (as the consultant) positively influenced Generative AI adoption factors. This case study highlighted that the co-experimentation created a synergistic environment for experimentation involving *"ChatGPT for Business Reference Materials for Early-Stage Entrepreneurs"*. This collaboration enabled more effective technology experimentation and resulted in the co-creation of business reference materials that combined AI-generated outputs, professional expertise, and research-based facts.

- **Co-creation and Experimentation for AI Adoption in Libraries**—Exploring how collaboration between librarians and entrepreneurs accelerates AI-driven service innovations. It also presents a case study of the University of Toronto (UofT) Libraries, focusing on how they are experimenting with AI technologies through incremental, small-scale, and strategic initiatives. Additionally, it proposes a structured approach to AI adoption in libraries, driven by need-based implementations, curiosity-driven explorations, or the combination. The libraries should foster a culture of experimentation, viewing failure as part of the process, and encouraging collaboration to foster co-creation. Curiosity-driven AI experiments and need-based experiments can be fostered by involving frequent library services users, for instance entrepreneurs in experiments using Enhanced Business Value Calculator, aligning with the AI experimentation policy, subjected to the rigorous monitoring and evaluation to track progress and impact. A case study is provided on how the Enhanced Business Value Calculator tool was applied in a collaborative experiment between a public library, a university library, and the most frequent users of *"ChatGPT for systematic literature reviews"* (on a trial basis). The objective of this experimentation was to determine whether Chat-GPT could be adopted in libraries for offering systematic literature review services. Another case study based on real consulting experience is presented which highlights how one of the librarians applied the curiosity-based experimentation (CBE) approach to assess a video-to-text AI tool, formulate a business case, and provide evidence-based recommendations for its adoption.

- **AI Experimentation Policy, Monitoring and Evaluation (M&E), and Ethical Considerations**—Presenting the AI experimentation policy for libraries involved in experimenting with AI technologies to ensure responsible AI integration in libraries, ensuring ethical AI initiatives that comply with regulations and protect data privacy. The policy balances innovation with responsible experimentation, focusing on areas that provide the most business value. Additionally, the study incorporates Monitoring and Evaluation (M&E) mechanisms to assess AI experiments and provide structured reporting. By documenting insights, libraries can refine AI adoption strategies, improve decision-making, and drive continuous advancements in business services through data-driven learning. AI experimentation reporting template, based on the documentation of a text-to-video experimentation conducted in one of the libraries is also provided. It serves to illustrate how to report detailed experimentation outcomes to library managers, aligning with the existing M&E framework in place at libraries and supporting both summative and formative evaluations.
- **Practical AI Technologies for Business Support Services**—Identifying and assessing low-cost, accessible AI solutions, such as ASReview, Connected Papers, and Citation Gecko, that libraries can integrate into business support services with minimal technical expertise. Libraries and entrepreneurs can collaborate to explore AI's potential, experiment with tools, and develop usage guides. Librarians can also enhance entrepreneurs' information literacy, respond to business queries using AI, and offer tailored training and workshops. The ready-to-use reference instructional materials on these AI technologies are also provided, which libraries can use internally for experimentation and adoption, or offer directly to their patrons as instructional resources for independent use.

This book is also driven by the idea that innovation in libraries is not limited to urban or well-funded institutions—it is a process accessible to any library willing to experiment, engage its users, and embed reflective practices like monitoring and evaluation. By offering practical frameworks and practice-based examples, the book seeks to empower librarians and library managers worldwide to position their institutions as active agents in their local innovation ecosystems.

Potsdam, Germany   Varun Gupta

Acknowledgements This research was funded by several sources, including the European Union's Horizon 2020 research and innovation programme (Project ID: 101061516, Acronym: LibrarIN), the Spanish National Research Programme RTI2018-101473-B-100, and Winning Scientific Management, Portugal, which co-funded two projects (Project IDs WIN-BUSMOD001 and WINBUSMOD007/2023). Additional support was provided by the Faculty Research and Innovation Grant at Gisma University of Applied Sciences, Potsdam, Germany (Project ID: RGVG_02, Acronym: DIGEnt). Detailed funding support is acknowledged in the funding acknowledgment section of the book.

The research was primarily conducted at

(a) Multidisciplinary Research Centre for Innovations in SMEs (MrciS) at Gisma University of Applied Sciences, Germany, and
(b) Universidad de Alcalá (UAH), Alcalá de Henares (Madrid), Spain.

It was also partly conducted at

(a) University of Toronto, Ontario, Canada, and
(b) University of Leicester, Leicester, UK.

The author would like to express my sincere gratitude to these esteemed institutions for their invaluable support throughout this research. Their contributions have been instrumental in making this work possible. Also, sincere gratitude to the academic and public libraries for their collaborative efforts in this research. The research collaboration has allowed for meaningful exploration and application of innovative approaches, contributing significantly to the development and impact of this work. Their expertise and resources were invaluable in realizing the objectives of this research.

Competing Interests The author has no competing interests to declare that are relevant to the content of this manuscript.

Funding Acknowledgements

The research received financial support from multiple sources, including **European Union's Horizon research and innovation programme** (Project ID: 101061516, Project Acronym: LibrarIN), and the **Spanish National Research Programme** RTI2018-101473-B-100. Additionally, **Winning Scientific Management, Portugal**, co-funded two projects under Project IDs WIN-BUSMOD001 and WINBUSMOD007/2023. Further support came from the **Faculty Research and Innovation Grant** at Gisma University of Applied Sciences, Potsdam, Germany (Project ID: RGVG_02, Project Acronym: DIGEnt).

This publication solely reflects the views of the authors, and the funding agency cannot be held responsible for any use that may be made of the information contained therein. The funder had no involvement in the execution of the study protocol and reporting, including data collection, analysis, decision to publish, or preparation of the manuscript communicating research findings.

Overview of the Book

- Investigates the business support services of different libraries, both academic and public, how they collaborate with other business support actors, and how they support entrepreneurs.
- Examines how co-creation between libraries and entrepreneurs strengthens generative AI adoption factors, leveraging them through collaborative experimentation to support informed adoption or switching decisions.
- Presents practical, real-world cases illustrating how libraries have applied AI technologies and experimentation to strengthen business support services.
- Provides AI experimentation policy, AI experimentation reporting template, and business case templates tailored for library environments.
- Includes reference instructional guides for AI tools (ASReview, Connected Papers, Citation Gecko) usable by librarians or directly by their patrons.
- Offers practice-based examples that libraries can adopt or adapt for providing business support services, conducting need-based or curiosity-driven AI experimentations in co-creation with patrons and business support actors, and integrating Monitoring and Evaluation for formative and summative evaluations through structured outcome reporting.

About This Book

This book investigates how libraries, both academic and public, support entrepreneurs by providing a range of business support services in collaboration with other business support actors. It describes the services offered and explores opportunities for innovating library services through the integration of artificial intelligence (AI) technologies and structured experimentation. A central emphasis is placed on co-creation between librarians and entrepreneurs, examining how collaborative AI experimentations actively strengthen adoption factors for Generative AI tools. Through this partnership, libraries and entrepreneurs jointly assess the value of AI tools, making informed decisions about adoption, refinement, or switching to alternative solutions.

The book explores two practical experimentation approaches: Need-Based Experimentation (NBE), driven by identified service gaps or operational objectives, and Curiosity-Based Experimentation (CBE), which encourages exploratory trials of emerging AI tools based on professional interest and opportunity. By combining these approaches, which have synergistic effects, libraries can foster a balanced culture of responsible innovation, further enhanced through co-creation with patrons and other business support actors.

Drawing on real-world cases from diverse libraries, it offers adaptable, practice-based examples for providing business support services, conducting AI experimentations, and integrating Monitoring and Evaluation (M&E) for both formative and summative assessments through structured outcome reporting. To operationalize these insights, the book provides AI experimentation policies, structured reporting templates, and business case formats to support ethical experimentation, evidence-based technology decisions, and impact evaluation of experiments. It also includes practical instructional guides for accessible AI tools like ASReview, Connected Papers, and Citation Gecko, which libraries can use themselves or offer directly to patrons.

This book is also driven by the idea that innovation in libraries is not limited to urban or well-funded institutions—it is a process accessible to any library willing to experiment, engage its users, and embed practices like monitoring and evaluation for serving the needs of their patrons. Altogether, this book serves as both a scholarly contribution and a practical guide, equipping libraries to strategically adopt AI, strengthen entrepreneurial as well as traditional services, and position themselves as active collaborators within their local innovation ecosystems.

Contents

About the Author

Varun Gupta received his Doctorate (cum laude) in Organizational Engineering, Doctorate (International/European Doctorate, Cum Lade) in Economics and Business Management, as well as a Doctorate in Computer Science and Engineering. He also earned his MBA (General), Máster en Dirección Internacional de Empresas, Master of Technology (By Research) in Computer Science and Engineering, and Bachelor of Technology (Hons.) in Computer Science and Engineering.

He is a Professor of Digital Innovation and Director of the Multidisciplinary Research Centre for Innovations in SMEs (MrciS) at Gisma University of Applied Sciences, Potsdam, Germany. He is also a researcher at Universidad de Alcalá (Spain). Previously, he was associated with University College London (UCL), London (UK), University of Toronto (Canada), Leicester University (UK), Software Engineering Research Group (SERG), Lund University (Sweden), Sapienza Università di Roma (Italy), Free University of Bozen-Bolzano (Italy), University of South-Eastern Norway (Norway), Poznań University of Technology (Poland), Uniwersytet Szczeciński (Poland).

Professor Gupta is the Editor-in-Chief of the International Journal of Computer Aided Engineering and Technology, a Scopus-indexed journal published by Inderscience Publishers. He also serves as an Associate Editor for IEEE Access, an SCIE-indexed journal published by the IEEE, and for PeerJ Computer Science, an SCIE-indexed journal published by PeerJ. He is a former editorial team member of the British Journal of Educational Technology (BJET) (an SCIE-indexed publication of Wiley), PLOS One (an SCIE-indexed publication of PLOS), and the Journal of Cases on Information Technology (ESCI and Scopus-indexed publication of IGI Global).

Professor Gupta has worked on multiple projects supported by various agencies such as the European Union and the Spanish National Programme. Additionally, he is included in the Stanford/Elsevier Top 2% Scientists List 2025. His areas of interest include evidence-based software engineering, innovation management, digital transformations and innovation, technology adoption in SMEs, entrepreneurship, and international business management.

Introduction

1

1.1 Research Background

Libraries have long served as critical enablers of entrepreneurship, offering essential business support services such as includes research guides and business consultations (Klotzbach-Russell et al. 2021; Hoppenfeld et al. 2013), business-specific workshops (Liu 2021), access to books, journals, and bibliographic databases (Hoppenfeld et al. 2013; Feldmann 2015; Franks and Johns 2015), business-related lecture series (Pryor 2014), research consultations, connections to external community business support agencies (Griffis 2015), and resources such as printers, Wi-Fi, and meeting rooms (Franks and Johns 2015; Faulkner 2018). Both public and academic libraries play a pivotal role in economic development through partnerships, digital literacy initiatives, and inclusive service models (Bishop et al. 2016; Cole and Stenström 2020; Baluk et al. 2020). These institutions foster an environment conducive to innovation and business growth.

The evolving digital landscape, particularly advancements in artificial intelligence (AI), presents new opportunities for libraries to enhance their service offerings (Chen 2023; Cox and Tzoc 2023). Generative AI technologies, such as ChatGPT, have emerged as potential tools for improving library operations for its patrons (Echedom and Okuonghae 2021; Winkler and Kiszi 2021; Ajani et al. 2022), for instance by supporting the instructional content creation, reference assistance, research support, digital literacy programs, information retrieval, search optimization, metadata extraction and creation, indexing, classification, content development, teaching, collection management, data and information literacy promotion, and even language translation (Johnson 2024; Adetayo 2023; Chen 2023; Cox and Tzoc 2023; Lund and Wang 2023; Lappalainen 2023; Yang and Mason 2023; Marshall and DuBose 2024; Formanek 2024; Torres 2024; Lund 2024). However, despite the recognized potential, research on AI adoption within libraries

V. Gupta, *Libraries as Hubs for Entrepreneurship*, Synthesis Lectures on Information Concepts, Retrieval, and Services, https://doi.org/10.1007/978-3-032-03569-1_1

remains limited, particularly concerning librarians' and entrepreneurs' perspectives to foster business support services.

Existing literature on AI adoption in libraries does not sufficiently address its application in business support activities. Additionally, there is a lack of structured experimentation, and monitoring and evaluation (M&E) frameworks to guide AI adoption in libraries. These frameworks should leverage co-creation between librarians and entrepreneurs while aligning with ethical norms and regulations, especially data privacy, necessitating well-defined AI experimentation policies. The AI experimentations should be planned and conducted in a way that also enables librarians to systematically assess experimentation outputs and outcomes through M&E. The co-creation—a collaborative approach involving librarians and entrepreneurs—has not been adequately explored in the context of AI-driven business support services.

Additionally, the literature highlights the gap in integrating user-friendly, low-cost AI solutions that require minimal technical expertise but can still provide significant value in entrepreneurial support. Addressing these gaps will provide libraries with clear pathways to effectively integrate AI-driven tools and optimize their role in supporting entrepreneurship. Existing literature does not report the accessible, user-friendly, and free technologies that could be useful for the libraries to innovate their business support services. There is a notable gap in the literature regarding the adoption of simple, cost-effective tools that can help libraries offer tailored services, particularly considering the technology adoption challenges, with resource constraints being a key factor.

Library managers play a crucial role in integrating emerging technologies like AI into library services, particularly in the context of supporting entrepreneurship. As key decision-makers, they are responsible for overseeing the adoption of AI tools, ensuring that these technologies align with the library's strategic objectives while managing resource constraints. Their expertise in managerial informatics is essential for navigating the complexities of AI implementation, from addressing ethical concerns to fostering collaboration between librarians and entrepreneurs. By combining managerial acumen with technological understanding, library managers can lead efforts to innovate business support services and enhance the library's role in economic development.

Adoption of emerging technologies in libraries today requires a collaborative effort involving both library staff and the continuous involvement of library managers. While staff members focus on the day-to-day implementation and user interaction with these technologies, library managers play a critical role in guiding the strategic direction. They help foster co-creation between librarians and patrons, promote a culture of experimentation, and establish robust monitoring and evaluation (M&E) frameworks. By aligning technology adoption with organizational goals, addressing resource constraints, and ensuring ethical compliance, library managers facilitate the successful integration and continuous improvement of AI-driven solutions in library services.

Library managers are also directly involved in AI experimentations, especially in small and medium size libraries, ensuring that these initiatives are aligned with library goals, and play a key role in promoting the development of innovative library support services. Throughout this book, the term 'librarians' will be used to encompass both library staff and library managers. This is because, given the collaborative nature of business support services and the evolving nature of AI technologies, both librarians and library managers play integral roles in the adoption and implementation of AI-driven solutions, working collaboratively in structures that resemble flat organizational models.

These research gaps underscore the need for a comprehensive study to examine AI adoption models, identify key influencing factors from both librarians and entrepreneur perspectives, propose structured experimentation and M&E frameworks, and practical AI technologies with business value to the libraries to foster service innovation.

1.2   Motivation

The motivation behind this research stems from the growing focus of the libraries in supporting the entrepreneurs and opportunities to leverage emerging technologies, especially AI technologies into their business support services. While libraries increasingly serve as facilitators of entrepreneurial activities, they often lack the necessary technological infrastructure and expertise to effectively implement AI-driven solutions, due to the evolving nature of these technologies and associated ethical concerns. The study aims to bridge this gap by examining AI adoption through an interdisciplinary lens, incorporating co-creation, experimentation, and M&E practices.

Furthermore, the rapid advancements in AI necessitate a deeper understanding of its implications for libraries. While AI offers numerous benefits, including enhanced efficiency and accessibility, it also presents challenges such as result inaccuracies, data protection concerns, privacy risks, accessibility barriers, biases, and ethical dilemmas pose significant obstacles (Nah et al. 2023; Panda et al. 2024; Nehra and Bansode 2024; Sanchez-Ramos et al. 2023; Elali and Leena 2023; Day 2023; Ray 2023; Gravel et al. 2023). By exploring the factors influencing AI adoption among librarians and entrepreneurs, this study seeks to provide actionable insights that will enable libraries to harness AI's full potential while mitigating associated risks.

1.3   Problem Statement

This book explores how libraries support entrepreneurs, emphasizing the adoption and experimentation with artificial intelligence (AI) technologies to strengthen and expand these services. Libraries play a crucial role in fostering entrepreneurship by providing access to bibliographic literature, research resources, and digital tools. However, despite the growing body of scholarly work on AI integration in libraries, existing research lacks empirical studies that examine AI adoption specifically within the context of business support activities.

Key research gaps include the absence of a structured AI adoption model that incorporates perspectives from both librarians and entrepreneurs while integrating co-creation and experimentation. Additionally, there is a need for a comprehensive AI experimentation policy that includes monitoring and evaluation (M&E), structured reporting, and ethical guidelines to ensure responsible AI adoption in libraries.

While literature acknowledges AI's transformative potential, it fails to provide actionable frameworks to guide AI-driven library services for entrepreneurs. Moreover, there is a lack of insights into user-friendly, cost-effective AI technologies that libraries can implement to bridge the gap between theoretical knowledge and practical business applications.

This study addresses these gaps by exploring the factors influencing AI adoption in libraries, analyzing the role of co-creation and experimentation in technology adoption, and developing a structured AI experimentation policy. By doing so, the research aims to provide actionable insights that enable libraries to leverage AI effectively while mitigating associated challenges such as data privacy concerns, accessibility barriers, and ethical considerations.

1.4   Research Objectives

The primary objective of this research is to investigate AI adoption in libraries for enhancing library business support services and to investigate how these libraries are supporting the entrepreneurs. The study aims to achieve the following sub-objectives:

RO 1.   To examine the role of libraries in supporting entrepreneurship.

RO 2.   To investigate AI adoption factors from both librarians' and entrepreneurs' perspectives.

RO 3.   To investigate co-creation and experimentation to drive AI adoption in libraries and enhance library business support services.

RO 4.   To develop a Comprehensive AI Experimentation policy ensuring M&E, structured reporting, and ethical implementation of AI experimentations.

RO 5.   To identify practical AI technologies that can be integrated into library services to enhance entrepreneurial support.

1.5   Research Questions

The research is guided by the following research questions:

- **RQ 1. How do libraries currently support entrepreneurship?**
  Library business support services are well documented in the literature (*refer to* Chap. 2). However, as academic and public libraries continue to innovate their approaches to entrepreneurship support, further investigation is needed to understand how these services evolve in response to technological advancements. Examining successful cases of library-driven business support can provide valuable insights into best practices that could benefit the peer libraries. This will help libraries refine their role in fostering entrepreneurship, ensuring their services remain relevant and impactful in an increasingly digital and AI-driven landscape.

- **RQ 2. What factors influence the adoption of AI technologies among librarians and entrepreneurs?**
  The successful adoption of generative AI in libraries can be significantly accelerated by understanding the key factors driving its integration among both librarians and entrepreneurs. Identifying these factors from the perspectives of both groups is essential for fostering a strategic, co-creation-driven approach to AI adoption. Examining these adoption drivers will strengthen the responsible use of AI, allowing libraries to better support entrepreneurs while also empowering entrepreneurs to apply their expertise with the AI technology under experimentation to help libraries experiment with and implement the technology. To the best of the authors' knowledge, no research has yet developed or empirically validated a model specifically for Generative AI adoption, providing insights into how entrepreneurs make adoption or switching decisions. Additionally, while the literature on AI adoption in library, there remains a significant gap in empirical studies examining the factors influencing librarians' decisions to adopt or transition to other Generative AI technologies to enhance their business-support services.

- **RQ 3. How can co-creation and experimentation introduce new ways to drive AI adoption in libraries to enhance business support services?**
  The limited insights in existing literature regarding AI experimentations in libraries, along with the lack of comprehensive frameworks and synergies, highlight a significant research gap. Exploring how co-creation can facilitate AI adoption in libraries is essential to address this gap. Co-creation enables the active engagement of stakeholders with librarians, including entrepreneurs, in designing and implementing AI solutions, ensuring that the technologies meet the diverse needs of users. This collaborative approach fosters more relevant and effective AI tools for business support services, helping librarians and their patrons to collaborate in AI experimentations. By investigating the experimentations and integration with co-creation, this research will uncover innovative pathways to enhance AI adoption in libraries, driving more impactful and sustainable integration to better support entrepreneurial communities.

- **RQ 4. What key considerations should an AI experimentation policy include to ensure effective Monitoring and Evaluation (M&E), structured reporting, and the ethical execution of controlled AI experimentations in library business support services?**

  The AI experimentation policy should empower librarians to explore AI technologies freely in areas where sensitive data is not involved, while implementing stricter controls for experiments that do handle sensitive data, ensuring full compliance with privacy and ethical standards. Libraries have been actively engaging in monitoring and evaluation (M&E) for various initiatives, such as the Libraries Build Business (LBB) program by the American Library Association (ALA), funded by Google.org. However, existing literature does not offer comprehensive AI experimentation policy that allows librarians to conduct experiments involving both sensitive and non-sensitive data. This includes conducting experimentations, documenting outcomes of evaluations of these experimentations and ensuring compliance with AI policies as part of M&E. In other words, there is a clear gap in scholarly literature regarding the development of an AI experimentation policy that not only fosters AI experimentation but also integrates M&E frameworks to assess the outputs and outcomes. This would support continuous improvements in experiments, ultimately enhancing library services.

- **RQ 5. Which AI technologies could offer the practical applications for enhancing business support in libraries, and how can they be effectively utilized to innovate and optimize these services?**

  The existing literature largely overlooks the potential of easily accessible, user-friendly, and free-to-use AI technologies currently available in the market that could significantly enhance library support for entrepreneurial communities. These technologies, which are often underutilized, hold great promise in addressing the diverse and evolving needs of entrepreneurs. By making these tools more widely available, libraries can provide more inclusive and effective services to entrepreneurs, for instance conducting M&E, literature reviews, reference services, etc. As such, there is a need for further exploration into how these accessible technologies can be integrated into support programs, thereby amplifying the impact of services designed to foster innovation and growth within entrepreneurial ecosystems.

1.6   Contribution of the Book

This research It makes significant contributions across multiple dimensions—theoretical, methodological, and practical. Specifically, it offers the following contributions:

Theoretical Contributions

The research study highlights the evolving role of libraries in supporting entrepreneurship. Key contributions include the idea of university libraries as open innovation partners, where their vast resources and expertise foster global entrepreneurship by providing access to the global network of entrepreneurial libraries, branding, market research, demand validation and competitor positioning. Additionally, it highlights the growing role of libraries, particularly university libraries, in fostering entrepreneurship through the strategic use of social networking sites (SNS). Libraries provide valuable market research that supports startups in their efforts to expand globally. By leveraging SNS, libraries help entrepreneurs form and maintain key partnerships, offering ongoing support for globalization. Finally, by examining cases from the University of Toronto (UofT) libraries, Baker Library of Harvard University, Public Library of Toronto (Toronto Reference Library (TRL)), and some of the public libraries funded under the American Library Association's (ALA) Libraries Build Business Program initiative, the research highlights the resources provided by these libraries for the entrepreneurs to foster entrepreneurial growth. This work showcases how libraries serve as key stakeholders in the entrepreneurial ecosystem.

In addition to exploring this, the research contributes to the existing body of knowledge by addressing critical gaps in the innovation of library business support services through AI adoption and controlled experimentation, Co-creation aligned with the AI experimentation policy and M&E. This is achieved in multiple ways as outlined below.

- The study proposed Generative AI adoption models by incorporating the perspectives of both librarians and entrepreneurs individually, addressing a key gap in the existing literature. Specifically, a new Generative AI adoption model from the entrepreneur perspective was proposed and then empirically validated. Then, the model was adapted to libraries offering business support services and empirically evaluated from the librarians' viewpoint. The study emphasizes the dual approach of examining Generative AI adoption from both entrepreneurs' and librarians' perspectives. This approach fosters a holistic understanding of adoption factors, encouraging co-creation and knowledge exchanges between the two stakeholders. Such collaboration helps overcome adoption barriers, with libraries benefiting from business expertise to address resource limitations, while entrepreneurs gain support from libraries in overcoming their challenges.
- The study did the comprehensive exploration of AI technology adoption in libraries through the lens of experimentation-driven frameworks. It advances the understanding of how libraries can transition from the initial hype surrounding AI technologies to a more strategic, practical implementation approach, exemplified by the case of University of Toronto (UofT) libraries.

  Two experimentation frameworks were proposed namely need-based and curiosity-based experimentation frameworks. By integrating them together, the study uncovers the synergy between these two forms of innovation and their impact on AI adoption. The proposed experimentation-driven frameworks offer a structured pathway for libraries to embrace technological advancements in series of small and incremental experiments that are designed and executed in a way that aligns with their unique needs and the broader business environment.

Furthermore, the study proposed the enhanced Business Value Calculator - a novel tool that measures the impact of library services innovations on entrepreneurs and businesses, highlighting the strategic role libraries can play in fostering innovation. The insights provided by the tool fosters co-creation in experimentations and promoted technology adoptions. This contribution not only enriches the theoretical foundations of AI adoption in libraries but also provides actionable insights for practitioners looking to leverage AI technologies in service delivery.

- A key aspect of this research is the development of an AI experimentation policy, ensuring that AI-driven initiatives are conducted ethically, in compliance with existing regulations, and with strict data privacy protections. This policy establishes guidelines for responsible experimentation, balancing innovation with data privacy while enabling libraries to explore AI technologies in a safe and structured manner, starting with the areas which provides maximum business value.
- Additionally, the study incorporates Monitoring and Evaluation (M&E) mechanisms to systematically assess AI experimentations and provide structured evaluation outcome reporting. By documenting insights from past experiments, libraries can refine AI adoption strategies, improve decision-making, and drive continuous advancements in business support services based on data-driven learning from previous experiments. This book is among the first to integrate the M&E framework with AI technology experimentations, ensuring systematic assessment, structured reporting, and continuous refinement of AI-driven initiatives in libraries.
- A key theoretical contribution of this book is the identification of AI technologies, such as ASReview, Connected Papers, and Citation Gecko, that libraries can integrate into business support services with minimal technical expertise. These technologies have been adopted in libraries as the outcome of the real-world consulting projects, and based on the lessons learned, actionable implementation guidelines are provided for peers to adopt these technologies effectively.

Methodological Contributions

The methodological contributions of this book stem from its innovative approach to studying AI adoption in libraries for entrepreneurial support. By integrating mixed research methods, including surveys, case studies, and practical experiences from consulting projects, the study bridges the gap between academic research and real-world applications. Given that this topic is still emerging in research, the book provides a structured methodological foundation that future studies can build upon. Below are the key methodological contributions:

- The book employs a combination of surveys, case studies *(including practical experiences from consulting projects)*. This mixed-methods approach enhances the depth and applicability of findings, providing both quantitative and qualitative insights into AI adoption in libraries offering support to the businesses. This research incorporates practical lessons from real consulting projects, making the findings more applicable to practitioners in libraries and business support ecosystems. Finally, the book examines real-world case studies from University of Toronto Libraries, Baker Library at Harvard, Public Library of Toronto (Toronto Reference Library (TRL)), and some of the public libraries funded under the American Library Association's (ALA) Libraries Build Business Program initiative, providing a structured method for analysing and adapting best practices across different library environments.

- A new Generative AI adoption model is proposed, outlining key factors influencing librarians' and entrepreneurs' decisions to integrate AI tools, offering a practical roadmap for successful AI implementation. This model differs from the other technology adoptions, for instance AI-driven Social Networking Sites used by librarians offering business support services.

- A methodological framework is introduced to guide libraries in conducting AI experimentations. This framework helps identify key areas for AI integration *(AI Experimentation Policy)*, assess outcomes systematically, and refine implementations based on practical findings *(M&E outcome reporting)*. The book also introduces structured curiosity-based and need-based AI experimentation frameworks, providing libraries with systematic approaches to test and implement AI technologies, leveraging synergies that exist between them.

- The book provides a structured monitoring and evaluation (M&E) process for documenting AI-related experiments in libraries. This ensures that AI adoption is not just trial-and-error but follows a systematic approach for assessing impact and making data-driven improvements.

- The study blends library science, managerial informatics, technology (AI research), entrepreneurship, Monitoring & Evaluation, and innovation management to create a holistic methodological approach. This interdisciplinary perspective enables a broader understanding of how AI-driven innovations can transform library services thereby innovating business support services.

- This research follows well-defined study protocols, ensuring methodological rigor and compliance with ethical standards. All research activities were conducted after securing approvals from institutional review boards, reinforcing adherence to ethical guidelines, data protection policies, and responsible research practices. The study protocols outline structured procedures for participant recruitment, data collection, and analysis, ensuring transparency and replicability. By formulating and rigorously adhering to these protocols, this research establishes a replicable framework for conducting responsible and transparent scholarly inquiry in the subject area.

Practical Contributions

This book offers several practical contributions, particularly at the intersection of libraries, entrepreneurship, and artificial intelligence (AI) adoption. The findings from the included studies provide actionable insights for library professionals, entrepreneurs, policymakers, and researchers seeking to leverage libraries as entrepreneurial support hubs, enhance AI-driven services, and optimize co-creation initiatives. The practical contributions are mentioned below.

- The research examines successful case studies from University of Toronto (UofT) Libraries, Baker Library at Harvard University, Public Library of Toronto (Toronto Reference Library (TRL)), and some of the public libraries funded under the American Library Association's (ALA) Libraries Build Business Program initiative. These examples offer valuable lessons that peer libraries can adapt to develop their own business support programs.
- The book provides insights into key factors influencing AI adoption among librarians and entrepreneurs. The analysis of these adoption factors, investigated individually for both groups, suggests that libraries can create a collaborative environment involving their patrons and external innovation actors. By strengthening these adoption factors, libraries can support both librarians and entrepreneurs in experimenting with AI technologies. Through continuous experimentation and evaluation, they can make informed adoption or switching decisions based on rational assessments of AI's effectiveness.
- The book presents a structured approach to AI adoption through experimentations, combining need-based implementations (AI adoption triggered by the specific organizational needs and strategic objectives) with curiosity-driven explorations (open-ended exploration of AI technologies driven by intrinsic motivation and discovery of the librarian). This balance ensures both practical impact and continuous learning within libraries.

   Libraries should cultivate a culture of experimentation, embracing failure as part of the learning process, allocating appropriate resources, and promoting open communication among librarians and external collaborators. Librarians who engage in AI experimentation driven by curiosity can have a positive impact on AI experimentations aimed at addressing urgent library needs. In turn, need-based experimentation can further ignite librarians' curiosity, encouraging them to explore new technologies independently. To support these initiatives, libraries could identify frequent users (as indicated by an enhanced business value calculator) and involve them in these experiments. Ultimately, these experiments will require libraries to establish a clear AI experimentation policy and implement outcome reporting through monitoring and evaluation (M&E) to track progress and impact.

- A structured AI experimentation policy framework is explained to help library managers determine which areas of library operations can benefit from AI experimentation without raising privacy concerns. This includes identifying commonly accessed library tasks where AI can enhance efficiency while ensuring patron data protection. Areas requiring access to patron data need to be subjected to the controlled experimentations.

The research provides practical insights about the AI experimentation policy and its implementation in libraries. The implementation requires librarians to identify the frequent tasks and assessing data sensitivity, and then using appropriate approach, Proactive Optimization, Controlled Experimentation, Opportunistic Experimentation, and Conservative Approach. It also emphasizes the need for institutional arrangements, including collaboration with legal and IT teams, and the creation of knowledge-sharing platforms. Training for librarians is highlighted as essential, focusing on data privacy, ethical AI practices, and risk assessment. The study also provides practical insights about formulating the M&E frameworks for its integration into AI experimentation, ensuring continuous assessment and improvement.

- Librarians are provided with a template for systematically recording and analysing AI experiment results as the part of M&E. This ensures that successful AI applications can be refined and expanded, while ineffective ones can be modified or discontinued. Library managers can also use these evaluations to make informed decisions about future AI initiatives. This template ensures consistent documentation and reporting of experimentation results, enabling peer learning from both successes and failures. It also supports library management in verifying compliance with approval conditions and enhances Monitoring and Evaluation (M&E) processes. This offers actionable recommendations for library managers to improve further AI initiatives by integrating monitoring and evaluation (M&E) activities.
- One of the major practical contributions of this book is the identification of easily accessible, low-cost AI solutions that libraries can integrate into their business support services without requiring significant technical expertise, for instance Active learning for Systematic Reviews (ASReview), Connected Papers, and Citation Gecko technology. Additionally, the ready-to-use reference instructional materials on these AI technologies are also provided, which libraries can use internally for experimentation and adoption, or offer directly to their patrons as instructional resources for independent use.

Entrepreneurs and libraries can collaborate to explore AI technologies, identifying their potential use cases and areas where these technologies outperform existing solutions. Librarians can experiment with AI, integrate these tools into library resources, and develop technology usage guides for patrons. They can also enhance entrepreneurs' information literacy and self-experimentation skills, respond to business-related information queries using AI, and provide tailored training and workshops.

Entrepreneurs, in turn, can contribute their expertise alongside functional specialists to support librarians in experimenting with AI, assessing the functional capabilities of these tools, and validating their accuracy across various input scenarios. This collaborative research will help libraries adopt AI-driven innovations, ultimately enhancing their services to better support entrepreneurs.

These contributions offer direct, actionable steps that library managers can take to integrate AI into their services, support entrepreneurs, and make informed decisions about AI experimentation and implementation.

Theoretical Background

2

Libraries serve as key enablers of entrepreneurship by providing essential business support services, including access to information resources, consultation programs, and collaborative networks. Both public and academic libraries contribute to economic development through partnerships, digital literacy initiatives, and inclusive service models.

As technology advances, artificial intelligence (AI), especially generative AI, is increasingly recognized as a transformative tool for enhancing library operations and expanding service capabilities, although research in this area is still evolving. Despite these advancements, gaps remain in understanding AI adoption within libraries, particularly from the perspectives of librarians and entrepreneurs. Existing research has not investigated the factors influencing AI adoption among librarians and entrepreneurs—an area of study that could help strengthen these factors and foster co-creation.

AI adoption should not be seen as a one-time decision but rather as a series of small, interrelated experiments, driven by co-creation and supported by monitoring and evaluation (M&E) activities. While the literature acknowledges AI adoption in libraries, it fails to examine these technologies specifically in the context of business support activities, through the lens of co-creation, M&E, and structured experimentation. Additionally, the existing literature largely overlooks the potential of easily accessible, user-friendly, and free-to-use technologies available in market in enhancing this support to meet the diverse needs of entrepreneurial communities.

This review synthesizes research on library business support, AI adoption for enhancing business support services, the identification of practical AI technologies suitable for libraries, and the integration of M&E in technology experimentation—identifying critical areas requiring further investigation as outlined in upcoming sections.

© The Author(s), under exclusive license to Springer Nature Switzerland AG 2026   13
V. Gupta, *Libraries as Hubs for Entrepreneurship*, Synthesis Lectures on Information
Concepts, Retrieval, and Services, https://doi.org/10.1007/978-3-032-03569-1_2

(a) Library support for the Entrepreneurs

The support provided by university and public libraries in fostering entrepreneurship has been documented by several authors (Parker et al. 2005; Underwood 2009; Hoppenfeld et al. 2013; Pryor 2014; Feldmann 2015; Griffis 2015; Franks and Johns 2015; Mehra et al. 2017; Faulkner 2018; Toane and Figueiredo 2018; Klotzbach-Russell et al. 2021; Liu 2021; Owolabi et al. 2022; Shehata and Eldakar 2023). Public libraries provide business support services that promote local economic growth (Bishop et al. 2016), foster community development (Cole and Stenström 2020; Scott 2011), enhance digital literacy (Baluk et al. 2020), and promote inclusivity (Scott 2011), often in collaboration with peer libraries and innovation ecosystem actors.

The support provided to entrepreneurs includes research guides and business consultations (Klotzbach-Russell et al. 2021; Hoppenfeld et al. 2013), business-specific workshops (Liu 2021), access to books, journals, and bibliographic databases (Hoppenfeld et al. 2013; Feldmann 2015; Franks and Johns 2015), business-related lecture series (Pryor 2014), research consultations, and connections to external community business support agencies (Griffis 2015). Additionally, libraries offer resources such as printers, Wi-Fi, and meeting rooms (Franks and Johns 2015; Faulkner 2018). Entrepreneurs utilize public library services to access business information (Owolabi et al. 2022), and libraries are encouraged to innovate by embracing the role of information facilitators (Stanikūnienė et al. 2023).

In addition to being information facilitators, libraries must secure the necessary resources to offer business support programming for entrepreneurs. Challenges may arise due to resource limitations, particularly financial constraints (Underwood 2009), and the need for librarians with expertise in business support (Shehata and Eldakar 2023). Librarians can support entrepreneurs, including underrepresented groups such as veterans with disabilities (Hoppenfeld et al. 2013).

Libraries offer business support services by collaborating with external business support agencies and peer libraries (Griffis 2015; Faulkner 2018; Klotzbach-Russell et al. 2021; Feldmann 2015). These partnerships can play a crucial role in enhancing inclusive and diverse business support services by leveraging each other's expertise and resources.

Entrepreneurship librarians must possess specialized competencies, such as research services and outreach, market and industry research, and innovation and problem-solving skills, to effectively support businesses (Toane and Figueiredo 2018). In an era of rapidly evolving technological innovations, librarians must reskill to experiment with emerging technologies, adopt them for valuable use cases, and innovate business support services. For example, with the growing emphasis on AI, librarians need to develop competencies to experiment with various technologies, select the most valuable ones, and create useful instructional materials for their patrons. This requires transforming organizational processes and fostering an experimentation culture within libraries. This approach aligns with Lo (2024a) suggestion that successful AI reskilling for librarians demands continuous learning, adaptability, collaboration, and hands-on practice.

Further investigation is crucial as universities and libraries continue to innovate their approaches to business support, particularly in the context of technological advancements. Examining successful support cases can offer valuable insights into best practices and the potential for scaling these services, helping to refine and expand the impact of business support initiatives. Further, the level and types of business support offered by academic and public libraries may vary, influenced by differing institutional priorities and the roles of library managers. Examining these differences can provide valuable insights into how these libraries could create the synergy by collaborating together to strangthen the effectiveness of business support initiatives.

(b) **Adoption of Artificial Intelligence Driven Technologies by Entrepreneurs and Librarians for Innovating business support services: Adoption Models, Co-Creation, and Experimentations**

AI in Libraries

To remain relevant in an ever-evolving business landscape, libraries continuously enhance their services by forming strategic partnerships with innovation stakeholders, integrating emerging technologies, and developing dynamic capabilities (Farney 2021; Ippoliti et al. 2021). At the heart of this transformation is digital innovation, which enables libraries to meet the changing needs of their patrons (Farney 2021; Ippoliti et al. 2021). Technological advancements not only enhance the accessibility and utilization of library resources but also contribute to improved performance (Khan et al. 2023). Libraries' digital transformation efforts may include the adoption of social media platforms to enhance engagement (Chu et al. 2012), the integration of AI-driven applications to improve services (Chen 2023; Cox and Tzoc 2023), and the implementation of augmented reality technologies to enrich user experiences (Kannegiser 2022).

The integration of AI technologies in academic libraries is expanding rapidly and is expected to continue growing (Winkler and Kiszi 2021). Evidence of this trend is reflected in a study by Hervieux and Wheatley (2021), which found that 43% of surveyed academic librarians in Canada and the USA express optimism about AI's positive impact on libraries, highlighting increasing awareness and interest. Similarly, research by Yoon et al. (2022) on public and academic libraries in North America indicates that while perceptions of AI are generally favourable, there is a strong demand for additional training in AI-related applications. Lo (2024b) also reports that library staff, despite having a basic understanding of AI, recognize its potential benefits. Meanwhile, Kaushal and Yadav (2022) found that key stakeholders are largely supportive of AI-driven tools, such as chatbots, further underscoring the growing acceptance of AI in library environments.

AI has the potential to significantly enhance library services for patrons (Echedom and Okuonghae 2021; Winkler and Kiszi 2021; Ajani et al. 2022). One prominent example is the rising adoption of Generative AI, particularly ChatGPT, which is reshaping library operations (Chen 2023). In cataloging, for instance, ChatGPT can assist in generating accurate records that adhere to metadata standards such as the Dublin Core Metadata Element Set (Brzustowicz 2023).

Studies by Johnson (2024), Adetayo (2023), Chen (2023), Cox and Tzoc (2023), Lund and Wang (2023), Lappalainen (2023), Yang and Mason (2023), Marshall and DuBose (2024), Formanek (2024), Torres (2024), and Lund (2024) have shown that ChatGPT can support a wide range of library services, including instructional content creation, reference assistance, research support, digital literacy programs, information retrieval, search optimization, metadata extraction and creation, indexing, classification, content development, teaching, collection management, data and information literacy promotion, and even language translation.

While AI offers significant opportunities to enhance library services, its adoption also comes with notable limitations that may constrain its practical application. Challenges such as result inaccuracies, data protection concerns, privacy risks, accessibility barriers, biases, and ethical dilemmas pose significant obstacles (Nah et al. 2023; Panda et al. 2024; Nehra and Bansode 2024; Sanchez-Ramos et al. 2023; Elali and Leena 2023; Day 2023; Ray 2023; Gravel et al. 2023). Lo (2024b) notes that while library staff possess a foundational understanding of AI and recognize its potential benefits, their ability to implement AI-driven solutions remains limited due to the need for further training and the establishment of ethical guidelines. Similarly, Kaushal and Yadav (2022) found that although stakeholders generally support AI tools such as chatbots, they remain cautious, particularly regarding privacy concerns and AI's effectiveness in managing complex tasks. Huang (2024) reports that although librarians acknowledge AI's growing role in the future of library services, they also emphasize that real-world challenges continue to impede its full-scale implementation. These challenges can deter librarians from experimenting with AI, either due to reluctance or the need for substantial resource investment and specialized expertise to properly assess AI's impact and reliability. These practical limitations have influenced the pace of AI adoption in libraries.

AI Experimentations in Libraries

Libraries seeking to integrate emerging technologies into their operations should base adoption decisions on ongoing experimentation. Instead of implementing technology all at once, conducting small-scale, incremental trials allows for learning and refinement. Each experiment builds on previous insights, with successful ones paving the way for broader implementation and unsuccessful ones offering valuable lessons for future testing. Even if a technology is not ultimately adopted, the iterative approach deepens libraries' understanding, encourages further experimentation, and nurtures a culture of innovation. Collaborating with patrons, particularly entrepreneurs, can further enhance these experimental efforts.

AI experiments should be carefully designed and conducted to not only identify potential use cases that add value to the library but also to address AI limitations, as highlighted by Nah et al. (2023), Panda et al. (2024), Nehra and Bansode (2024), Sanchez-Ramos et al. (2023), Elali and Leena (2023), Day (2023), Ray (2023), and Gravel et al. (2023). Key themes in AI policies include ethics, transparency, balancing innovation with regulation, and data privacy, all of which libraries must integrate into their AI-driven operations (Lo 2023). Libraries have actively engaged in AI regulatory developments, such as contributing to ethical frameworks (Bradley 2022). The AI experiments must align with ethical norms and regulations, with a strong emphasis on data privacy. The AI experimentation policy should allow librarians to freely explore AI technologies in areas where sensitive data is not involved while enforcing stricter controls for experiments that do, ensuring compliance with privacy and ethical standards. To the best of the authors' knowledge, the existing literature does not provide information on an AI experimentation policy that enables librarians to conduct AI experiments with both sensitive and non-sensitive data while documenting outcomes and ensuring adherence to AI policies as part of monitoring and evaluation (M&E). To the best of the author's knowledge, the existing literature provides limited information on how AI experimentations are conducted across various libraries, the frameworks used to guide such experiments, and the synergies between these frameworks. This gap in knowledge highlights the need for more comprehensive studies that explore the practical application of AI in libraries, the development of standardized experimentation frameworks, and how these frameworks can work together to foster effective and ethical AI integration.

Toane and Figueiredo (2023) suggested that libraries need to experiment with new ideas, activities, or method with minimal commitment at smaller scale rather at larger one. Many services started as small tests before becoming permanent. Trying new things helps libraries improve and show users they are open to innovation. It also gives staff confidence to explore creative solutions. Cooper suggests planning experiments carefully, setting clear goals, and learning from both successes and failures. Even if an idea does not work, it can still provide useful lessons for the future. To the best of the authors knowledge, the literature provides any experimentation framework that guides the AI driven experimentation in libraries.

Librarians who consistently engage with emerging technologies through experimentation develop dynamic capabilities that support the adoption of valuable innovations—both present and future—while enhancing library services for patrons. According to Lo (2024a), effective AI reskilling relies on fostering a culture of continuous learning, adaptability, and collaborative exploration. A hands-on, practical approach strengthens librarians' ability to navigate the rapidly evolving AI landscape. By gaining direct experience and working collaboratively with new technologies, librarians cultivate essential competencies, including dynamic capabilities, which drive ongoing experimentation with emerging tools while reducing susceptibility to industry hype. Liu et al. (2024) highlights the critical link between AI adoption, existing dynamic capabilities, and AI adaptation. Their findings suggest that well-developed dynamic capabilities are key to recognizing AI opportunities, leveraging them effectively, and transforming operations to support activities such as business model innovation. Regular AI experimentation further enhances librarians' ability to detect new opportunities, capitalize on them, and reallocate resources efficiently, reinforcing their capacity to lead future AI initiatives within libraries.

Staying informed and actively engaging with technological advancements allows librarians to keep both themselves and their patrons up to date on new developments. This includes offering guidance on technology use, understanding its capabilities and limitations, addressing related concerns, and establishing best practices (Akakpo 2023; Fruehauf, Beman-Cavallaro and Schmidt 2024). By taking on this role, libraries position themselves as key facilitators of responsible and informed engagement with Generative AI (Bridges 2024).

AI Adoption Models from Librarians and Entrepreneur Perspective

Understanding the functional capabilities and limitations of the technology through the continuous experimentation depends on reinforcing the factors that drive technology adoption, for which identifying these factors from the users' perspectives, especially librarian's and entrepreneurs' perspective is important. The adoption can be fostered by reinforcing adoption factors through increased interaction with technology, for instance, by promoting technology experimentation culture in libraries, getting support from patrons such as entrepreneurs, for instance, by promoting co-creation between patrons and librarians and getting assistance from the innovation ecosystem, such as prompt engineering training provided by companies.

It essential to investigate generative AI adoption factors among librarians. Understanding these factors can foster the responsible adoption of emerging technologies, helping libraries support their patrons effectively and solidify their role as key players in the innovation ecosystem. This investigation will enable libraries to better assist their patrons, ensuring they are equipped to navigate and leverage new technologies responsibly and effectively. Additionally, investigating adoption factors from the entrepreneur's perspectives will help to understand the factors that fosters adoptions thereby helping them to strategically adopt these technologies. Understanding the adoption factors in librarians and entrepreneur's context will help to strengthen the adoption factors thereby leading to strategic adoptions driven by co-creation based continuous incremental experimentations among them.

Fruehauf, Beman-Cavallaro, and Schmidt (2024) highlighted the University of South Florida (USF) library's collaborative approach, where interdisciplinary teams worked together to provide patrons with AI-related information for frequently asked queries. This case underscores the importance of academic and public libraries expanding their professional networks and fostering ongoing discussions about emerging technologies. By doing so, libraries can raise awareness, facilitate experimentation, integrate new learnings, and identify practical applications of AI. The adoption of such technologies requires interdisciplinary perspectives to drive meaningful innovation within library settings.

One effective strategy for fostering innovation in libraries is co-creation. Research suggests that co-creation enhances managerial innovation capabilities (Frow et al. 2015), reduces uncertainties associated with evolving technologies and user needs (Pillar et al. 2011), and enables organizations to navigate uncertain times through innovation. In this collaborative process, library users do not merely benefit from services but actively contribute knowledge and insights, leading to creative and practical solutions. This approach strengthens relationships between librarians and patrons, encourages innovation, and ensures that solutions align with diverse needs and expectations. By engaging patrons in AI experimentation, libraries can gain valuable user-driven insights that inform their innovation strategies. The collaboration between librarians and users not only enhances experimentation practices and dynamic capabilities but also fosters the continuous evolution of library services, ensuring they remain relevant and impactful.

Research on AI adoption has introduced new models, such as the Task-Oriented AI Acceptance (T-AIA) model (Yang et al. 2022) and the Artificial Intelligent Device Use Acceptance (AIDUA) model (Gursoy et al. 2019), while also extending existing frameworks like the Technology Acceptance Model (TAM) and the Unified Theory of Acceptance and Use of Technology (UTAT) (Kelly et al. 2023).

Kelly et al. (2023) reviewed 60 studies on AI adoption across six sectors—customer service, education, healthcare, organizations, consumer products, and others. Their findings indicate that researchers primarily used extended versions of TAM and UTAT, incorporating additional variables to explore AI-related factors. However, the AIDUA model has yet to be expanded.

Gursoy, Chi, Lu, and Nunkoo (2019) introduced the AIDUA model, which outlines three-stage process customers go through before either accepting or rejecting AI technologies. They argued that traditional models like the Technology Acceptance Model (TAM) were not designed to examine the adoption of AI-driven customer service systems that function without human involvement. According to the AIDUA model, AI adoption unfolds in three phases: primary appraisal, secondary appraisal, and outcome. In the primary appraisal stage, individuals assess the significance of AI technology, influenced by factors such as social norms, hedonic motivation, and anthropomorphism. The secondary appraisal stage involves a careful evaluation of the benefits and drawbacks, particularly in terms of performance and effort expectancy. Finally, in the outcome stage, the emotions triggered in the secondary appraisal phase shape customers' willingness to embrace or resist AI technologies in service interactions. This framework has been widely applied to explore customer attitudes toward AI-driven service solutions, particularly in industries where AI is designed to replace human customer service representatives.

Yang, Luo, and Lan (2022) introduced the T-AIA model, arguing that the factors emphasized in the AIDUA model—such as social influence, hedonic motivation, and anthropomorphism—are more relevant to social-oriented AI devices than to task-oriented AI systems. They contended that the adoption of task-oriented AI devices depends primarily on their ability to help users achieve functional goals, such as problem-solving capabilities. Therefore, the decision to adopt these technologies should be driven more by their utilitarian value than by hedonic motivation. Like the AIDUA model, the T-AIA framework follows a three-stage adoption process: primary appraisal, secondary appraisal, and outcome. However, the key factors influencing adoption decisions differ. In the primary appraisal stage, utilitarian motivation, interaction convenience, and task-technology fit are crucial. The secondary appraisal stage is shaped by perceived competence and flow experience, while the outcome stage revolves around switching intention—whether customers choose to adopt AI systems or revert to human-provided services.

To the best of the authors knowledge, to date, no research has developed and empirically validated a Generative AI adoption model to offer insights into how entrepreneurs perceive its application in their startup environments. Furthermore, despite the expanding literature on AI adoption in libraries and the increasing role of libraries in assisting entrepreneurs, there remains a significant gap in empirical research on the factors influencing librarians' decisions to adopt or transition to Generative AI technologies in their business-support library services.

AI Technologies with Practical Applications for Libraries

Libraries play a crucial role in supporting entrepreneurs by constantly seeking technologies that can be adopted within their limited resources, while still delivering significant business value. However, the existing literature largely overlooks the potential of easily accessible, user-friendly, and free-to-use technologies in enhancing this support. There is a noticeable gap in the research regarding the adoption of simple, cost-effective technological tools that can empower libraries to offer tailored resources and services for entrepreneurs.

Literature lacks studies that report some practical technologies that could be adopted by peer libraries. These technologies, often overlooked, can provide valuable solutions for libraries looking to offer practical, scalable support, particularly for entrepreneurs in underserved communities or those with limited access to expensive technologies. By focusing on these technologies, especially AI driven technologies that require minimal technical expertise, libraries could not only foster a culture of innovation among entrepreneurs but also help bridge the digital divide and resource limitations that often hinder their adoptions. Yet, the literature has not sufficiently addressed how libraries can incorporate these easy-to-use technologies into their service models to meet the diverse needs of entrepreneurial communities.

(c) **Monitoring and Evaluation of AI Technology Adoption Experiments for Innovating Business Support Services**

The adoption of emerging technologies, such as Generative AI, requires librarians to approach their interactions as a series of small, continuous experiments. These experiments help librarians gain a thorough understanding of the technology's capabilities and limitations, allowing them to identify potential use cases for business support services. It is essential to continuously monitor and evaluate the outcomes of these experiments to measure their effectiveness and impact. This evaluation process will assist library managers in making informed decisions about whether to continue, scale up, adopt specific use cases, or refine the experiments further.

When viewing experimentation as part of a library's Digital Transformation program, frameworks like the Theory of Change (Weiss 1995) and logic models can be used to illustrate how experimental activities lead to the desired outcomes over short, medium, and long-term periods, including successful use cases identified and implemented post-experimentation round, confidence gained by librarians in conducting experimentations, business growth or economic development. These models are essential for effective planning and evaluation of library programming, and initiatives like technological experimentations (Sullivan and Stewart 2006; Erica Breuer et al. 2015; Savaya and Waysman 2005; Bucher 2010).

Public libraries are shifting their focus from merely offering services to creating a meaningful impact on their communities (Dunn 2021). To achieve this, their services must be evaluated to measure their effectiveness. The evaluation results will highlight the extent to which library programs have positively influenced the community. Matthews (2017) emphasizes the essential need for libraries to evaluate their services, highlighting a shift from basic service provision to proving their value through measurable impact. By adopting a range of quantitative and qualitative tools, libraries can assess both traditional and customer-centric outcomes, creating a comprehensive understanding of their service effectiveness.

Various approaches for assessing the impact and performance of libraries are outlined in the literature (Urquhartand 2018; Yim et al. 2020). For instance, according to Poll and Payne (2016), libraries should adopt outcome-based evaluations to showcase the effectiveness and value of their services. Public libraries significantly contribute to the monitoring and evaluation of initiatives focused on achieving the SDGs by offering critical information and resources that support these efforts (Aregbesolaa et al. 2023).

The concept of M&E is not new to libraries, as it has been well-documented in literature, with many libraries already conducting M&E activities. For example, 13 public libraries participated in the Libraries Build Business (LBB) initiative, supported by Google.org and led by the American Library Association (ALA). This project aimed to strengthen libraries' efforts in promoting small business success. ALA and these libraries worked with Cicero Group to create an M&E framework, and the evaluation results showed that these initiatives were timely, relevant, and had a positive impact on their communities (American Library Association 2023). Apart from the publicly available report of the ALA reports to the best of the authors information, the M&E concept for evaluating the AI technology experimentations for the libraries, including those providing business support services, had not been reported in the scholarly literature.

Decisions regarding technology adoption should be based on strategic planning, allowing libraries to align their goals with external trends and facilitate the integration of AI technologies to improve services (Saunders et al. 2015). When technology adoption is not prioritized in strategic planning, it often leads to lower implementation rates (Okunlaya et al. 2022). Embedding AI adoption within strategic planning is essential, as it should prioritize fostering a culture of continuous experimentation. This includes embracing lessons from failures, encouraging the sharing of both successes and challenges, and actively supporting the piloting of new initiatives, even on a small scale. To make each round of experimentation more data-driven, libraries should integrate Monitoring & Evaluation (M&E) into their strategic plans. This will enable them to assess the impact of technology adoption, refine strategies based on evidence, and ensure that innovations meet user needs effectively by learning from previous experiments and analyzing their results and impacts. A robust M&E framework fosters data-driven decision-making, helping libraries not only track progress but also adapt strategies dynamically amid continuously evolving technological landscape.

This book aims to address key research gaps across multiple themes, including library business support services, AI adoption in libraries, and the adoption of AI technologies specifically in the context of business support activities from both librarian and entrepreneur perspectives. It will explore these aspects by incorporating co-creation, monitoring and evaluation (M&E), and structured experimentation as integral components of AI adoption. Furthermore, this research seeks to identify practical AI technologies that offer significant value to libraries, ensuring their effective implementation in business support services while fostering innovation and collaboration. Table 2.1 highlights the research gaps as addressed by this book.

Table 2.1 Research gaps addressed by the book

S. No.	Theme	Research gaps
1.	Library support for the entrepreneurs	• Universities and libraries continue to innovate their approaches to business support, particularly in the context of technological advancements. Examining successful support cases can offer valuable insights into best practices and the potential for scaling these services, helping to refine and expand the impact of business support initiatives, necessitating further investigations
2.	AI adoption in Libraries offering business support services, focusing on the following: • AI Adoption model from Librarian and Entrepreneur perspectives • AI adoption drive by Co-creation and Experimentations • M&E of AI experimentations • An AI experimentation policy that fosters controlled experiments with both sensitive and non-sensitive data while integrating monitoring and evaluation (M&E)	• Literature acknowledges AI adoption in libraries; it fails to examine adoption of these technologies specifically in the context of business support activities from both librarian and entrepreneur perspectives • Literature does not examine AI experimentations incorporating co-creation, monitoring and evaluation (M&E), and structured experimentation outcome reporting as integral components • The existing literature offers limited insights into how AI experimentations are conducted in libraries and the frameworks that guide them • Evaluating the AI technology experimentations for innovating library business support services had not been reported in the scholarly literature • The existing literature does not provide information on an AI experimentation policy that enables librarians to conduct AI experiments with both sensitive and non-sensitive data while documenting outcomes and ensuring adherence to AI policies as part of monitoring and evaluation (M&E)
3.	AI technologies with practical applications for libraries	• The existing literature largely overlooks the potential of easily accessible, user-friendly, and free-to-use technologies available in the market in enhancing this support to meet the diverse needs of entrepreneurial communities

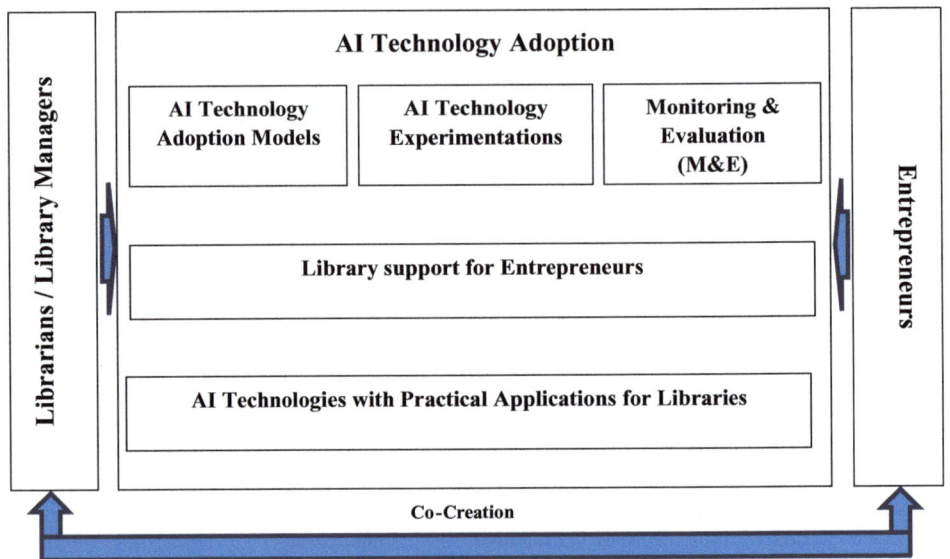

Fig. 2.1 Research areas addressed by the book

This book focuses on investigating key areas in the context of libraries offering business support services to entrepreneurs (Fig. 2.1). First, it examines the library support available to entrepreneurs, exploring the range of resources and services libraries provide, with particular attention to how these services address the needs of underrepresented and emerging entrepreneurial groups.

The study also delves into AI technology adoption, specifically analyzing adoption models from both the perspectives of libraries and entrepreneurs. This includes investigating the adoption of AI-driven technologies for strengthening the business support library services and the potential challenges and opportunities for both parties in implementing such innovations. A central theme in this research is co-creation, where libraries and entrepreneurs collaborate on AI experimentation, fostering a culture of innovation.

Additionally, the book explores the integration of monitoring and evaluation (M&E) to ensure the effectiveness of technology adoption experiments for continuous improvement of business support services through data-driven decisions. Lastly, the research examines the practical applications of AI technologies within libraries, focusing on tools that are easy to use, cost-effective, and accessible, with the potential to enhance library services and better support entrepreneurs in their business ventures.

Research Methodology

This chapter outlines the research methodology adopted to explore library business support activities and the role of AI adoption through experimentation and co-creation. The study aims to identify factors influencing AI technology adoption, including Generative AI, from the perspectives of both librarians and entrepreneurs. It also examines AI experimentation policies, the integration of monitoring and evaluation (M&E) in AI initiatives, and the creation of a structured outcome-reporting template. Furthermore, the research identifies practical AI tools that can enhance library business support services and investigates their effective implementation in libraries of any size. To support this, the study also provides ready-to-use reference instructional materials on these AI technologies, which libraries can use internally for experimentation and adoption, or offer directly to their patrons as instructional resources for independent use. The study also includes real cases from libraries on various investigated topics, such as Curiosity-Based Experimentation (CBE), providing practical insights into actual library practices that peers can replicate or adapt within their own library contexts.

Given the absence of systematic academic inquiry in this area, this chapter provides rich insights about the use of mixed-methods approach in the research, combining case studies, surveys, and insights from consulting experiences with libraries actively engaged in AI-driven business support. This approach ensures the collection of empirical evidence on real-world practices, adoption challenges, co-creation dynamics, and M&E mechanisms, providing both theoretical contributions and actionable recommendations for library innovation.

© The Author(s), under exclusive license to Springer Nature Switzerland AG 2026
V. Gupta, *Libraries as Hubs for Entrepreneurship*, Synthesis Lectures on Information Concepts, Retrieval, and Services, https://doi.org/10.1007/978-3-032-03569-1_3

Justification of Research Methods Employed

Theoretical background section of this book highlights the literature gaps that this research work bridges. It underscores that, despite the growing recognition of libraries as key players in business support, academic literature remains largely silent on how these institutions can leverage AI for such initiatives. While various universities and libraries, particularly in the United States of America and Canada, have been offering business support services and have also begun integrating AI into these initiatives, these efforts are not systematically documented or analysed in scholarly research. Existing studies acknowledge AI adoption in libraries but do not address its application in business support activities, nor do they examine AI-driven co-creation, experimentation, and structured outcome evaluation as integral components. There is also limited insight into how AI experiments are conducted in libraries and the frameworks that guide them. Furthermore, the literature does not provide a comprehensive AI experimentation policy that enables librarians to conduct controlled trials with both sensitive and non-sensitive data while ensuring adherence to ethical and regulatory standards through systematic M&E. Additionally, research has largely overlooked the potential of accessible, user-friendly AI tools that could enhance library services in supporting entrepreneurs.

Given the lack of well-documented studies, this research adopts a mixed-methods approach that combines case studies *(including practical consulting experiences),* and surveys with the libraries actively engaging in business support. When an area is under-explored in academic literature, relying solely on theoretical models or secondary data for multidisciplinary areas at the intersection of AI technology, experimentation, policy, and M&E is insufficient; empirical evidence is needed to understand real-world implementations and challenges.

Case studies will help document successful practices, providing a basis for understanding how libraries have integrated AI into their business support initiatives. Surveys will capture perspectives from both librarians and entrepreneurs to identify key adoption factors, co-creation dynamics, and barriers to AI integration, as they have been using these technologies in both their professional and personal lives. Additionally, for investigating some areas like library business support services, the data collected in case studies through interviews at the libraries was supplemented with data collected through secondary sources.

The study also incorporates findings from consulting experiences *(essentially case studies with data from real participation in the projects)* with libraries that were supported in strengthening their AI-driven business support services through co-creation, experimentation, AI experimentation policies, M&E, and the implementation of practical technologies aligned with the library's operational context. These firsthand experiences contribute to the literature and provide practical insights for libraries of any size that are offering or planning to offer support to entrepreneurs. Additionally, these insights are applicable to libraries seeking to improve services for other patron groups, given the synergies between entrepreneurial support and general library services.

Beyond identifying adoption factors and co-creation mechanisms, the study contributes to the development of an AI experimentation policy by proposing a structured framework tailored for libraries, based on real-world consulting experiences. The research provides a framework for conducting AI trials, ensuring controlled experimentation with proper documentation and adherence to ethical guidelines. The study also develops an outcome-reporting template, requiring AI experimentations to be subjected to M&E to systematically evaluate outcomes and refine AI-driven services. Furthermore, it identifies practical AI technologies that libraries of varying sizes can implement to enhance their business support services, bridging the gap between theoretical AI applications and real-world usability, based on consulting experiences.

Since academic literature has yet to explore AI adoption in library business support in a structured and empirical manner, this study fills that gap by providing real-world evidence. By integrating multiple research methods, it ensures a rigorous, practice-driven approach that captures both theoretical and applied dimensions of AI adoption in libraries. This comprehensive approach contributes to the broader discourse on library innovation, offering a foundation for future research and practical guidelines for libraries seeking to enhance their business support services through AI.

Consulting experience as a research method involves conducting a practical case study in real settings, where the outcomes are derived from firsthand insights and real-world applications, offering valuable practical insights as results.

Research Methods Addressing Each Research Question

The specific research methods employed to address each research question of the study are explained in this section. It explains how different methods together (mixed-methods research) were applied to gather relevant data and generate meaningful insights aligned with the study objectives.

RQ 1.   How do libraries currently support entrepreneurship?

Gupta and Rubalcaba (2021) based their research findings on practical experiences gained as part of a consulting project focused on the globalization of a Spanish startup in the U.S. market, with support from the academic sector, particularly the university library. The study follows a case study approach, where practical insights were drawn from the researcher's direct participation in the project. Data collection involved observations and engagements within the consulting process, providing firsthand insights into the role of academic libraries in supporting international market expansion of the businesses.

The research findings of Gupta et al. (2022) are based on consulting experiences with multiple startups and libraries, focusing on the use of social networking sites to provide business support services to entrepreneurs. The study follows a case study approach, drawing practical insights from direct participation in consulting projects that facilitated and examined the application of social networking sites for offering library business support services and formation and sustainability of collaborative partnerships between startups and libraries. Data collection involved observations and engagements with stakeholders, offering firsthand insights into the role of libraries in fostering entrepreneurship through digital platforms and strategic partnerships.

The research findings of Gupta (2023a) are grounded in a case study approach, drawing insights from publicly available data obtained through social networking sites, such as Facebook, and the official website of the University of Toronto's Mobile Application Development Lab (MADLab). The analysis focuses on understanding MADLab's role in supporting individuals affiliated with the university in mobile application development and its collaboration with UOT libraries in organizing training sessions and other events. The study received ethical approval from the Institutional Review Board of Gisma University of Applied Sciences, Potsdam, Germany, under protocol number 02/2023.

The research study to investigate the library support for the entrepreneurs follows a case study approach, involving data collection through interviews, secondary data from official websites, business support flyers posted on library notice boards, and other publicly available documents, for instance American Library Association's (ALA) Libraries Build Business Program initiative resources. The study investigates entrepreneurial support services offered by various libraries, particularly the University of Toronto (UofT) Libraries, Baker Library of Harvard University, Public Library of Toronto (Toronto Reference Library (TRL)), and some of the public libraries funded under the American Library Association's (ALA) Libraries Build Business Program initiative. For the research findings involving primary research, informed consent was obtained from librarians and other practitioners before data collection, ensuring no personal data was collected. The study received ethical approval from the Institutional Review Board of Gisma University of Applied Sciences, Potsdam, Germany, under protocol number 02/2023.

RQ 2.   **What factors influence the adoption of AI technologies among librarians and entrepreneurs?**

The research study conducted by Gupta (2025a) employs a survey to investigate the adoption of Generative AI among librarians offering business support. The survey process began with a pilot test involving 60 librarians from academic and public libraries worldwide, with 52 completing it (87% response rate). Following the research study protocol and guidelines from Gupta (2024a), participants assessed the clarity, neutrality, logical flow, and relevance of the questionnaire in capturing technology adoption factors. Their feedback helped refine the survey before full deployment.

The final survey was distributed to 219 librarians, yielding 176 responses (80% response rate) from 110 libraries globally. Participants, selected through purposive sampling, were librarians supporting businesses, including student entrepreneurs, with some experience in Generative AI. The survey included Likert-scale (1–5) questions and optional qualitative feedback. No personal data was collected, ensuring anonymity, and participants could edit responses or withdraw at any time. Data was securely stored in password-protected OneDrive for six months post-research.

For data analysis, the study employed Partial Least Squares Structural Equation Modeling (PLS-SEM) using SmartPLS 4, validating relationships between latent variables in the conceptual model. Quality assurance protocols ensured reliability, incorporating librarian-specific modifications from the pilot phase. Participants received clear instructions, and technical issues, such as lost survey access, were managed while maintaining privacy. The study strictly followed ethical guidelines, including informed consent, data security, and privacy protection, in line with the research study protocol (Gupta 2024a) and approval from the Institutional Review Board of Gisma University of Applied Sciences, Germany (protocol number 010424).

Another research study by Gupta (2024b) employs convenience and purposeful sampling, a non-probability approach, to examine entrepreneurs' adoption of Generative AI versus alternatives. Participants were selected from the researcher's professional and extended networks, including public libraries, universities, accelerators, and incubators. The sample consists of entrepreneurs who have used or considered using Generative AI, particularly ChatGPT. The study specifically excludes non-innovative SMEs, such as restaurants and bakeries, and instead focuses on startups offering disruptive products or services.

To ensure rigorous data collection, structured questions were distributed only after obtaining informed consent. The research study protocol, the University of Leicester's standard participant information sheet, the General Data Protection Regulation (GDPR) privacy notice, and an informed consent form were drafted and shared with the participants before data collection.

A total of 600 entrepreneurs were invited to participate, and each received the University of Leicester's standard participant information sheet, GDPR privacy notice, and informed consent form. Of these, 482 provided consent, resulting in an 80% response rate. The sample included co-founders as well. Surveys were conducted via Google Forms from January 10 to 19, 2024, following an information-sharing and consent phase from January 3 to 9, 2024. Participation was voluntary, and personal data were collected only for optional follow-ups, which were ultimately not requested.

Data were analyzed using Partial Least Squares Structural Equation Modeling (PLS-SEM), an approach suited for complex models, small sample sizes, and non-normal data distributions. The analysis followed two main steps: Measurement Model Assessment and Structural Model Assessment, which are detailed in the results section.

The conceptual model validated in this study is based on the Generative AI adoption framework proposed by Gupta and Yang (2024a). This model extends the Technology Acceptance Model (TAM) by integrating additional factors derived from the researcher's extensive professional experiences, and a comprehensive analysis of existing AI adoption models. The professional experiences include significant engagement with multiple small and medium-sized enterprises, and in-depth discussions with industry experts about GenAI and its adoption in business setting.

Ethical approval for the research was obtained from multiple institutions, Winning Scientific Management in Lisbon, Portugal (Protocol No. 0823 J), and University of Leicester Ethics Sub-Committee (study Design ID: 43,400). Additionally, the research received clearance from the UK Government's Academic Technology Approval Scheme (ATAS) under the Foreign, Commonwealth & Development Office (FCDO) on July 20, 2023.

To ensure data security, all collected information was stored in a password-protected OneDrive account provided by the university, with access restricted to the principal investigator. Participants could complete the survey at their convenience, ensuring minimal burden and ethical compliance. The study adhered to recognized ethical and data security standards while providing a robust methodology for analysing AI adoption among entrepreneurs. The study followed established research protocols (Gupta and Yang 2024b).

RQ 3.   How can co-creation and experimentation introduce new ways to drive AI adoption in libraries to enhance business support services?

The research study conducted by Gupta (2024c) employed a case study approach, collecting data from the Director of Strategic Initiatives and the Associate Chief Librarian for Science Research and Information at the University of Toronto (UofT) libraries through interviews and email correspondence. This was one of the areas identified as part of a two-week research visit in March and April 2023, during which other areas investigated pertained to Research Question RQ1. The research aimed to explore AI adoption strategies in libraries. Participants were informed about the study's objectives, and confidentiality was maintained throughout the research process. The data collected was systematically analysed using NVIVO software, applying thematic analysis to identify key patterns and strategies. The researcher's analysis of the information gathered from the Associate Chief Librarian was shared with her for review. Based on her feedback, minor edits were made to the analysed results to ensure that the researcher's interpretation of the collected and analysed data was accurate.

The research study conducted by Gupta and Gupta (2023a) involves the proposal of two experimental-driven AI technology adoption frameworks for libraries. The Need-Based Experimentation (NBE) and Curiosity-Based Experimentation (CBE) Frameworks are based on the author's professional experience and adoption patterns observed across ten university libraries. Real insights were drawn from consulting experiences and direct observations of AI adoption practices in these libraries, providing a practical foundation for the framework. These practical insights also helped explore the synergy between the two experimental-driven AI technology adoption frameworks proposed in another research study by Gupta and Gupta (2023b). They provided a deeper understanding of how the frameworks intersect and complement each other, offering libraries a powerful toolkit for navigating the complex landscape of AI technology adoption.

The research study by Gupta and Gupta (2023c) is based on practical insights acquired through a case study of the adoption of a real AI technology—video-to-text converter technology—in one of the libraries, driven by his curiosities to experiment with the technology. The study was conducted through case study research with observation, participation in the librarian's experimentation process, and a short interview. This approach allowed for a detailed understanding of how curiosity-driven adoption of AI technology unfolded in a real-world library setting. it was used to strengthen the library's social media presence and create a significant impact on its online community. Specifically, the experimentation involved the technology usage to produce videos for entrepreneurship events and was conducted for period of a month. The outcome of the experimentation was evaluated based on short-term Key Performance Indicators (KPIs), such as average time spent on the website per shared video and the number of likes, dislikes, and shares. These KPIs offered measurable insights into the impact of AI-generated content on user engagement. To gain deeper insights, the librarian was contacted for a brief interview at the conclusion of the experimentation. The interview focused on detailing the experimentation process, challenges faced, and key learnings gained through the adoption and application of AI technology in the library's operations.

Another research study by Gupta (2024b) is based on consulting experiences conducted with multiple libraries, using a practical case study approach to gather insights from real-world projects. The study leverages direct involvement with libraries to provide practical insights into the adoption of new technologies and service improvements. Consulting experiences allowed for an immersive approach, where the researcher actively participated in the enhancement of the Urban Libraries Council's business value calculator. This tool was refined by classifying library services and offering a comprehensive resource list for each category based on researcher's professional experiences with the library. The structure of the enhanced business value calculator is disseminated in

(Gupta 2023b). By engaging directly with libraries, the researcher observed and documented the process of co-creation with patrons, helping libraries drive experimentation-based technology adoptions. The consulting experience involves experimentation with Generative AI, specifically ChatGPT, to improve library operations. This initiative involved experimenting with ChatGPT to find it applicability to support systematic literature review and was organized by a public library in collaboration with an academic library and the academic departments of a nearby university. The findings from these consulting experiences offer actionable insights and best practices, derived from real-world application and experimentation, aimed at fostering technology innovation and improving library entrepreneurship initiatives.

The research mentioned in this section (RQ 3) received ethical approval from the Institutional Review Board of Gisma University of Applied Sciences under protocol number 02/2023.

RQ 4.   **What key considerations should an AI experimentation policy include to ensure effective Monitoring & Evaluation (M&E), structured reporting, and the ethical execution of controlled AI experimentations in library business support services?**

The research study conducted by Gupta (2024e) employs a qualitative action research approach, as existing literature does not provide direct insights into AI experimentation policies within library settings. The research is based on empirical insights gained through direct consulting experience with a library that systematically integrated ChatGPT through an incremental experimentation process. The study involved observing how the library explored potential AI use cases, identified areas for effective integration, and determined scenarios requiring more controlled and rigorous experimentation. The experimentation process was carefully designed to ensure privacy and security, fully exploring the AI applications to contexts that did not involve patron data allowing librarians to independently plan and executing these experimentations without needing prior approval from management, and subjecting experimentations involving personal data using controlled experimentation protocols. The findings from these real-world experiments contributed to the development of a structured AI experimentation strategy and controlled experimentation protocols. By adopting an iterative and reflective approach, the research ensured that the AI Experimentation Policy was informed by practical considerations, balancing innovation with ethical principles and regulatory compliance.

The research study conducted by Gupta (2024f) builds upon the same previous consulting project that informed the AI experimentation policy, adopting a qualitative research approach to explore the development of a standardized outcome reporting template for AI experiments in libraries. As existing literature does not provide guidance on standardized reporting for AI experimentation in library settings, this research relies on empirical insights gained from real-world applications. The consulting project involved working closely with the library to ensure that AI experimentation outcomes were consistently documented, facilitating peer learning, compliance verification, and integration with Monitoring and Evaluation (M&E) processes. The outcome template was designed to capture both successes and challenges, allowing libraries to refine their AI adoption strategies based on systematically recorded experiences. Given the absence of prior research on this topic, the practical experiences from this project serve as a validated research method, offering an applied framework for other libraries seeking to adopt AI through structured experimentation and M&E integration.

The research by Gupta (2024e, 2024f), received ethical approval from the Institutional Review Board of Gisma University of Applied Sciences, Germany, under protocol number 010424.

RQ 5.   **Which AI technologies could offer the practical applications for enhancing business support in libraries, and how can they be effectively utilized to innovate and optimize these services?**

The research study conducted by Gupta (2024 g) employs a qualitative research approach based on action research methodology, leveraging direct consulting experience with a library that integrated ASReview to enhance its reference services for entrepreneurs. Since existing literature does not explore AI-driven systematic review tools in library-based entrepreneurial support, the research relies on real-world application insights. The consulting project involved evaluating ASReview's effectiveness in streamlining systematic literature reviews for entrepreneurs seeking relevant information from bibliographic literature to support their business development. The methodology involved direct engagement with librarians and entrepreneurs, testing the tool's capabilities in providing literature recommendations, conducting workshops with the entrepreneurs, and providing hands-on sessions with the tool focused on real-world business challenges like value proposition innovation. Findings from this practical implementation were used to develop recommendations for libraries adopting AI-based systematic review tools to support entrepreneurial research, ensuring that the results were grounded in validated, real-world applications. The study received ethical approval from the Institutional Review Board of Gisma University of Applied Sciences, Potsdam, Germany, under protocol number 010424.

The research study by Gupta and Gupta (2023d) employs an applied qualitative research approach, drawing from professional expertise and real-world engagements with librarians and entrepreneurs. Given the absence of literature on systematic literature reviews within the entrepreneurial journey, the research methodology is based on practical experience using Connected Papers technology to assist entrepreneurs in navigating scholarly literature. The methodology included direct observations of entrepreneurs and librarians using Connected Papers to identify relevant literature to get business related information in response to the entrepreneur business related information query. The study received ethical approval from the Institutional Review Board of Gisma University of Applied Sciences, Potsdam, Germany, under protocol number 02/ 2023.

The research study by Gupta (2023c) follows an applied research methodology, leveraging empirical observations and consulting experience with library support for entrepreneurs. Given the growing role of libraries in providing research assistance, the study investigates how Citation Gecko technology can enhance systematic literature reviews and bibliographic research. The methodology involves analysing Citation Gecko's functionality, particularly its ability to map citation networks and generate visual research overviews, assisting both entrepreneurs and librarians in identifying relevant studies to meet the entrepreneur business related information needs from the bibliographic literature. By focusing on real-world applications rather than theoretical constructs, this research provides actionable insights into how libraries can integrate AI-driven tools to optimize research support services for entrepreneurs. The study received ethical approval from the Institutional Review Board of Gisma University of Applied Sciences, Potsdam, Germany, under protocol number 02/2023.

Libraries Support for the Entrepreneurs 4

This chapter aims to present the role of libraries in supporting entrepreneurship, by undertaking the case study of the business support services of University of Toronto Libraries, Baker Library at Harvard University, Public Library of Toronto (Toronto Reference Library (TRL)), and some of the public libraries funded under the American Library Association's (ALA) Libraries Build Business Program initiative. These libraries play a crucial role in supporting entrepreneurs by providing essential resources, industry insights, and technological tools to help them navigate the complexities of business development and growth—both through their own offerings and in collaboration with accelerators and other business support actors.

Insights from Consulting Experience: Case Studies in Library Support for Entrepreneurs

Gupta and Rubalcaba (2021) highlights the crucial role of university libraries in fostering entrepreneurship by integrating into open innovation ecosystems. These libraries have expanded their traditional functions beyond academic research and now provide valuable business support to startups, entrepreneurs, and small businesses. By leveraging their extensive global professional networks and the credibility of established academic institutions, libraries assist entrepreneurs in refining business models, identifying customer segments, and making data-driven market decisions.

One of the major contributions of university libraries to entrepreneurship is their ability to provide international market intelligence. Entrepreneurs seeking to expand beyond their national borders often struggle with market entry barriers, unfamiliar business environments, and the difficulty of identifying potential customers. Libraries bridge this gap by offering access to global business databases, economic reports, and analytical tools

© The Author(s), under exclusive license to Springer Nature Switzerland AG 2026
V. Gupta, *Libraries as Hubs for Entrepreneurship*, Synthesis Lectures on Information Concepts, Retrieval, and Services, https://doi.org/10.1007/978-3-032-03569-1_4

that enable startups to make strategic market expansion decisions with minimal effort. By leveraging their multinational academic and professional networks, libraries help businesses simulate product demand validation, understand regulatory landscapes, and adapt business models for different markets.

Gupta et al. (2022) highlights the significant trend in library business support through the increasing adoption of Social Networking Sites (SNS). Libraries have long used social media to engage with students and academic communities, but in recent years, they have extended these platforms to provide business-related services. SNS offer a real-time and interactive platform for libraries to support entrepreneurs, providing access to market insights, competitor analysis, and international business networks without requiring physical visits to library facilities. Through SNS, libraries enable startups to Crowdsource market intelligence by engaging with a broad audience of business experts, academics, and fellow entrepreneurs, gain access to international business data, including customer demographics, pricing strategies, and competitor activities, and form strategic partnerships with other businesses, investors, and mentors in foreign markets.

Libraries that have successfully integrated SNS into their business support services provide entrepreneurs with opportunities to identify key market trends, regulatory changes, and economic indicators. However, while some libraries have fully embraced SNS-driven business assistance, others still operate within traditional academic frameworks, limiting their ability to provide real-time, business-focused engagement.

Libraries are becoming essential strategic partners for startups by offering structured business support programs. Libraries and startups should initiate partnerships grounded in their specific needs, nurture and develop these collaborations over time, and periodically reassess and reshape them. As a result, such partnerships naturally progress through multiple stages of initiation, growth and adaptation. A key framework for these partnerships, as outlined by Kim et al. (2010), consists of a four-stage process encompassing the following steps:

- Identifying Strategic Needs—Startups must first define their long-term business goals and assess how library resources can support them. If a startup seeks only one-time assistance, such as accessing a report, the partnership may have limited value. However, if a startup requires ongoing market intelligence, business model validation, or international expansion strategies, then a long-term collaboration with a library becomes a valuable strategic asset.
- Selecting a Library Partner—Entrepreneurs evaluate potential library partners based on several factors, including the library's business expertise, level of engagement on social media, past collaborations with businesses, and availability of business resources. Libraries with strong social media presence and active involvement in business incubators or innovation hubs are more attractive partners for startups looking for business intelligence and networking opportunities.

- Implementation of Partnership—Once a partnership is formed, effective collaboration between startups and library staff is essential. This involves regular knowledge-sharing sessions, workshops, and personalized consultations where libraries provide guidance on customer identification, regulatory compliance, funding opportunities, and business research methodologies.
- Reassessing and Reshaping the Partnership—Over time, startups must evaluate the effectiveness of their collaboration with libraries. Metrics such as market traction, business expansion success, and the quality of insights gained from library resources help determine whether the partnership should continue, be modified, or be expanded.

Based on the preceding studies, several key takeaways can be identified. One of the clearest takeaways is the growing use of user-friendly technologies—especially social networking platforms—that enable libraries to deliver business support services in more interactive and scalable ways. These tools allow libraries to go beyond traditional information access, enabling real-time engagement, crowdsourced market insights, and global connections. For libraries aiming to support entrepreneurs, adopting such digital tools is not only a matter of convenience but also a strategic shift toward greater accessibility and responsiveness.

Another important takeaway is how librarians are innovating existing services to offer more knowledge-intensive responses tailored to entrepreneurial needs. Rather than simply pointing to resources or providing basic reference services, librarians are increasingly guiding entrepreneurs toward strategic directions—offering curated insights, comparative data, and targeted research support. Although the innovative use of existing library resources and staff competencies depends on the library's size and available resources, even small libraries can begin by offering basic reference services—if not knowledge-intensive support—laying the groundwork for future development. While these responses may not offer final solutions, they serve as valuable entry points for entrepreneurs to explore opportunities, validate ideas, and refine their business models. This shift highlights the library's evolving capacity to act as a trusted partner in the early stages of business development.

Finally, the cases underscore the importance of long-term, strategic partnerships—both with patrons and with external innovation actors. Libraries that establish structured, ongoing collaborations with startups or innovation hubs are better positioned to offer relevant, high-impact services. These partnerships require mutual commitment, regular communication, and clear metrics for evaluating success. As entrepreneurship becomes more integrated into library missions, such partnerships can provide the foundation for sustained innovation support.

Library Support for Entrepreneurs: Practical Case Studies

University of Toronto (UofT) libraries
The University of Toronto (UofT) libraries play an important role in entrepreneurship ecosystem of UofT. The ecosystem includes over 12 accelerators, Centre for Entrepreneurship, libraries across three campuses, and a specially designated Entrepreneurship Librarian role (Gupta 2024c). University of Toronto (UofT) has successfully established 650 companies, leading all Canadian universities this regard and attracting over \$3bn (CAD) in investments in the last ten years. In 2022, UBI Global acknowledged UofT's entrepreneurial efforts by placing it among the top 10 university-managed incubators worldwide.[1] The UofT library system is the largest research library system in Canada and the second largest in North America, providing unparalleled resources and support for their patrons, including their student entrepreneurs.[2]

UofT libraries support entrepreneurs at various levels and stages of their entrepreneurial journey, with more skills development oriented. They offer resources and services to help build entrepreneurship skills, including access to bibliographic databases, subscriptions, research tools, and entrepreneurship-focused workshops. These workshops range from introductory sessions to in-depth topics such as primary research, business model canvas development, patent searches, and data resources. Additionally, libraries provide access to 3D printing facilities. All resources and services are offered within the licensing agreements of the library, meaning they are primarily intended for academic purposes—such as skill development—rather than direct commercialization. The libraries' support and consultations guide entrepreneurs in finding the right resources to address their business needs rather than offering direct business advice.

UofT libraries also extend their services to events organized by the university's 12 accelerators. While some of these accelerators support entrepreneurs at all stages, including commercialization, libraries focus on skill development. Librarians participate in various entrepreneurship-related events, such as the annual Entrepreneurship Week, including sessions like "Innovating Together: The Power of a Supportive Women's Startup Ecosystem."

The UofT entrepreneurship ecosystem comprises 12 accelerators and other faculty-linked units that collaborate to foster entrepreneurship. Some accelerators, like BRIDGE, is a collaboration between the University of Toronto Scarborough (UTSC) Department of Management and the UTSC Library (https://www.utsc.utoronto.ca/thebridge/). Librarians provide entrepreneurship skill development support to students, faculty, and researchers through library resources, specialized programs, and expert guidance. While libraries do not directly support entrepreneurs seeking commercialization, they enhance skill-building efforts for patrons, including those seeking support from the accelerators. By offering research support and specialized tools, librarians help entrepreneurs hosted by these accelerators gain valuable insights. For example, librarians can assist with primary research

---

[1] https://research.utoronto.ca/inventions-commercialization-entrepreneurship/entrepreneurship-u-t.
[2] https://www.utoronto.ca/about-u-of-t/quick-facts.

tools, business model canvas design, or suggest relevant contacts for domain-specific queries.

The accelerators play a crucial role in commercialization by connecting entrepreneurs with external networks. For instance, UofT's Faculty of Arts & Science houses the Centre for Entrepreneurship, which provides coworking spaces, prototyping and makerspace facilities, brainstorming sessions, and a Venture Mentorship Service (VMS) (https://www.entrepreneurship.artsci.utoronto.ca/). VMS connects entrepreneurs with experienced industry mentors who offer free, confidential, and customized guidance.

Collaboration between libraries and accelerators strengthens entrepreneurship support at UofT. Accelerators could refer entrepreneurs to librarians for research assistance, while librarians contribute to joint programming initiatives, and could also refer their patrons to one of the accelerators. The entrepreneurial librarian at UofT serves as a central figure, coordinating efforts among faculty libraries, accelerators, and entrepreneurship centers. These librarians engage in regular discussions about programs, services, and events, ensuring continuous knowledge-sharing and support for the university's entrepreneurial ecosystem.

An advantage is that university students, researchers, and alumni can benefit from the combined support of libraries and multiple accelerators. For example, libraries—working in collaboration with accelerators—can help individuals build their entrepreneurship skills. When they are ready to further develop their ideas with the intention of commercialization, they can turn to accelerators for mentorship, funding, and access to specialized resources, depending on the nature of their business idea.

Gupta (2023a) reports the case of Mobile Application Development Lab (MAD-Lab), a facility established in 2013 at the Gerstein Science Information Centre at the UOT (https://mobile.utoronto.ca/). MADLab focuses to advance mobile software development and provides services exclusively for UOT-affiliated students, researchers, and faculty. MADLab provides a range of technology-driven services beyond app development, fostering entrepreneurship, collaboration, and digital innovation. MADLab offers mobile application development support, enabling students and researchers to develop and deploy apps. While funding for development depends on grants, the center provides free consultations, technical assistance, and matchmaking opportunities for students to collaborate on projects. It also supports UOT startups by offering legal services in partnership with legal professionals, including free 15-min consultations on intellectual property and business-related legal issues at various startup stages, from ideation to scaling.

The lab plays a vital role in connecting students with peers and startups, allowing them to gain hands-on experience in app development and engage with entrepreneurial ventures. Startups share their requirements, and MADLab disseminates these opportunities among the developer community, encouraging collaboration. In addition, MADLab is actively involved in community engagement, as seen in its response to the 2015 Chennai floods, where it used social media to mobilize support from the UOT developer network. Innovation at MADLab extends to crowdsourced app testing, where students and researchers provide user feedback to refine mobile applications. The lab also integrates with library services, offering resources such as 3D printing, entrepreneurial workshops, and digital literacy programs. Additionally, MADLab shares scholarship opportunities, hackathon details, keynote events, and emerging technology tools, such as X Code for prototyping.

MADLab and libraries collaborate in a mutually beneficial way to enhance the UOT community's access to entrepreneurial and library services. MADLab provides technical resources like 3D printers, scanners, and VR equipment, which support both library services and entrepreneurial activities. It also participates in library events, offering expertise in areas like 3D printing and data detox. MADLab helps libraries by supporting entrepreneurial skill development and directing startups to library resources. In return, libraries refer users to MADLab for technical assistance, app creation support, and event promotion, fostering a strong community for innovation and entrepreneurship.

Baker Library at Harvard Business School (HBS)
Baker library provides support to student entrepreneurs affiliated with HBS and other Harvard University units. This support is not intended to facilitate commercialization but rather to develop entrepreneurial skills, for instance referencing support, developing market research skills etc. Librarians offer different support to these entrepreneurs, for instance research expertise by guiding students on conducting primary research, identifying appropriate tools, determining the availability of publicly accessible data, and understanding customer identification methods. However, their role is to provide direction rather than business advice. Library resources, including subscriptions, are strictly for academic purposes. Users must sign a statement confirming that they will use these resources solely for academic purposes.

Baker Library's entrepreneurial support focuses on three key areas namely, **Harvard Innovation Labs**—Librarians offer research expertise, helping students navigate information sources relevant to their entrepreneurial endeavors, **Harvard Rock Center for Entrepreneurship**—Librarians provide support through summer internships and presentations on research resources that could be useful for students in their entrepreneurial journeys, and Startup Bootcamp—Held in January, this program equips students with essential startup skills, tools, and practices, emphasizing experimentation-driven methodologies. These centres and programs assist entrepreneurs in progressing from idea to commercialization. Librarians contribute by providing directional support, such as research guidance and referencing assistance, to aid students in their entrepreneurial process.

Alumni can also seek guidance from librarians, particularly for fact-finding tasks such as strategies to identify potential customers, locating relevant business data, or connections with alumni. While librarians do not establish direct connections between Harvard entrepreneurs and internal or alumni networks, they provide access to tools, technologies, and details of the alumni that could help entrepreneurs identify and engage with relevant networks using library-maintained information. Further, the librarian's involvement in teaching and learning support in HBS is instrumental in developing entrepreneurial skills and making students aware of the library programs and resources.

Toronto Public Library (TPL)

The Toronto Reference Library (TRL), largest public reference library in Canada and branch of Toronto Public Library (TPL) besides other library services to the patrons, offers a range of business support services to entrepreneurs. These free services include access to databases and online research tools, such as Canadian Business and Current Affairs (CBCA), resources such as book and periodical collections, financial newspapers, and historical Canadian company annual reports, business programs, including customised education programs for the adults group learners and schools related to starting the business and industry trends search, workshops, seminars, specialized resources, workspaces for meetings, networking opportunities such as TPL small business networking meetup group, and Digital Innovation Hub. The Digital Innovation Hub at the Toronto Reference Library offers access to computers with design software, scanners, printers, 3D design and printing tools, and studio space for film and audio production—empowering users to explore digital creativity and entrepreneurial projects. The library also offers the fee based services to the patrons for the customised research using the Library's print, microform and electronic resources (https://www.torontopubliclibrary.ca/intellisearch/).

Additionally, entrepreneurs can benefit from one-on-one consultations with business librarians *(called book-a-librarian)*. Book-A-Librarian service could be used to getting one-to-one assistance from the librarian, including reference service about library resources, business related queries, or support to get connected with external business support actors. These consultations provide valuable guidance on topics such as setting up a company in Canada, understanding tax structures, accessing library resources, connecting with external business support partners, and identifying relevant business materials available in the library.

A key initiative is the Entrepreneur in Residence program, an eight-week residency featuring seminars, workshops, and consultations with an entrepreneur selected as the resident for that year. The Entrepreneur in Residence reviews submitted business ideas and offers free one-on-one meetings with selected applicants to critique and evaluate their business ideas and plans. Throughout the residency, they also provide business support programs and personalized consultations.

To enhance its business support offerings, the library actively collaborates with external innovation partners, including entrepreneurs, business experts, and organizations such as the Toronto Business Development Centre. These partnerships help provide specialized support to entrepreneurs at various stages of their business journey.

Entrepreneurial Support in Public Libraries: Case Studies from the American Library Association's (ALA) Funded Libraries Build Business Program

American Library Association's (ALA) Funded Libraries Build Business Program initiative, funded by Google.org and led by the American Library Association (ALA), is a national program aimed at strengthening the role of public libraries in supporting entrepreneurship (https://www.ala.org/advocacy/workforce/grant). Launched in 2020, the program awarded funding grants of up to $150,000 to 13 public libraries across the United States, representing a diverse mix of urban, rural, and rural areas, to build local capacity, expand resources, and create inclusive support systems for entrepreneurs (https://www.ala.org/advocacy/workforce/grant). Apart from the individual programs offered by these libraries, the collaboration between these 13 public libraries also led to the co-creation of several valuable resources for the wider library community. These include practical artefacts such as a communications toolkit, monitoring and evaluation (M&E) resources—such as small business surveys, interview guides, Theory of Change frameworks, and M&E systems (Gupta 2025b), and a comprehensive Libraries Build Business playbook—all designed to support libraries looking to start or scale up their business support services. These tools offer actionable guidance on outreach, program design, impact measurement, and equity-centered practices, making them a valuable foundation for any public library irrespective of their size and budgets, aiming to empower local entrepreneurs through support services tailored to the unique needs of their communities, especially the underrepresented entrepreneurs.

The playbook highlights that the funded public libraries offered a wide range of support services, including business centers, makerspaces and Libraries of Things, workshops and classes, peer learning and networking opportunities, mentorship from business experts, one-on-one consultations, reference services, access to research databases and print collections, as well as self-paced courses (American Library Association 2022). These libraries supported small businesses through 1,210 events attended by 14,417 people (American Library Association 2023). Delivering these services effectively often relied on a combination of existing library resources, the expansion of current services for instance starting new business support programs or accelerator programs, and collaboration with external partners (American Library Association 2022). Each library developed and implemented innovative models to support local entrepreneurs—particularly those from historically underserved groups—through business training, access to resources, mentorship, and community partnerships using the ALA grants. Libraries have launched new business support programs, including those developed in partnership with external business support organizations, expanded existing programs for the underrepresented patrons, using their existing or their upgraded resources to better serve the community. Some examples of entrepreneurial support initiatives carried out by public libraries as part of the Libraries Build Business (LBB) program are discussed below.

- **Baltimore County Public Library (BCPL)** (https://www.bcpl.info/)
  Baltimore County Public Library (BCPL) offers a wide array of resources aimed at supporting entrepreneurs throughout their business development journey. These include access to experienced reference librarians who assist patrons in locating relevant information, as well as specialized tools for conducting market research, exploring industry trends, and gathering data necessary for making informed business decisions. Instructional materials and guides are also available to help users better understand the processes involved in starting and managing a small business.

  In addition to providing these resources, BCPL actively collaborates with other business support organizations, including Baltimore City's Enoch Pratt Free Library (EPFL) and professional business mentors from diverse fields. Through this partnership, the library co-organizes an initiative known as the Entrepreneur Academy (American Library Association 2022). This academy is an acceleration program composed of seven structured classes, each designed to cover a fundamental area involved in setting up and managing a business. The sessions address key basic topics such as business strategies, finance, market research, legal considerations, financial planning, taxation, marketing strategies, and the development of a business plan.

  What makes the program especially relevant is its delivery by professional business counsellors who bring practical, real-world experience to the classroom. The program is designed to be accessible to individuals at various stages of their entrepreneurial journey—whether they are exploring an idea for the first time or refining an existing concept. Participation in the accelerator program helps the participants to get introduced to the library business support services and the available resources. This will encourage the entrepreneurs to understand the basic but building concepts of starting the business, explore what the library has to offer and to integrate these assets into their business starting process. The goal of the academy is to support participants in drafting a comprehensive business plan that reflects both the knowledge gained from the sessions and the insights derived from independent research.

  By situating this program within the library setting and in partnership with other local institutions, the Entrepreneur Academy contributes to a broader effort to expand access to entrepreneurship education—particularly for those in communities that are underrepresented, for instance individual of colour, or communities with higher unemployment rates, and thus could benefit from gaining skills to start their own business. The initiative reflects an evolving role for libraries as facilitators of economic opportunity, using their space and networks to connect people with the expertise and tools they need to take concrete steps toward building a sustainable business.

- **Spokane County Library District** (https://www.scld.org/)

  The Spokane County Library District offered the **Small Business Boot Camp** program, designed to support local entrepreneurs and small business owners in Deer Park and surrounding areas (American Library Association 2022). This initiative provides monthly educational sessions led by industry experts, covering critical business topics such as planning, marketing, pricing, and branding. The program aims to equip participants with practical skills to help grow their businesses effectively. To make the program accessible, childcare services was offered during in-person sessions during one-year long program, allowing more entrepreneurs to participate. In addition to workshops, participants have the opportunity to receive micro-grants after the successful completion of the program, which can be used to invest in specific business improvements. The Boot Camp also encourages networking and connections with peers and the local business organizations, fostering a supportive entrepreneurial community.

  The program would have been instrumental in integrating library resources—such as personalized research assistance and access to library resources to gain better understanding of the library resources, and opportunity to use them for their business activities. Overall, the Small Business Boot Camp through trainings and microgrants would have been instrumental in placing these public libraries as vital hubs for business development and community economic growth in rural areas like Deer Park.

  The M&E conducted by the libraries through the M&E framework, as outlined in the American Library Association's final M&E report (American Library Association 2023), suggests among survey respondents, 88% felt more motivated, 82% more confident, and 52% more successful as business owners. Notably, 77% were women and 64% were Black, Indigenous, and People of Color (BIPOC). Overall, 68% said they were very likely to recommend the library's support.

Towards an Integrated Entrepreneurship Support Ecosystem

The library cases presented in the previous sections highlight several important realities:

(a) Entrepreneurs require a wide range of resources to turn their business ideas into practice—including skills development, funding, intellectual property protection, mentorship, and access to reliable data for informed decision-making. However, universities and public libraries often operate with limited resources, particularly in terms of funding and staffing. The most effective approach is to share resources, enabling collaborators to leverage each other's strengths while avoiding unnecessary duplication.

(b) External business support actors play a crucial role in expanding the scope of entrepreneurial services. It is unrealistic to expect libraries or universities to provide all specialized mentorship or tools in-house. Therefore, collaborations must be established, maintained, and sustained. Reference services that connect entrepreneurs to relevant external partners can be especially valuable.

(c) The role of librarians is key—even small libraries can reposition their existing patron services to support entrepreneurs using current resources. For example, libraries that offer research and market analysis training could adapt these services to assist aspiring entrepreneurs ("buddy entrepreneurs") in refining their business ideas.

(d) While tensions may arise between traditional and evolving librarian roles, entrepreneurship support initiatives offer an opportunity to promote existing resources, raise awareness of library services, and drive innovation. Expanding services to include business support—especially in collaboration with external partners—can enhance the library's relevance and impact. Collaborative initiatives can support the professional development of librarians, foster innovation in service delivery, and lead to meaningful enhancements of existing library resources.

Entrepreneurship support within universities has evolved beyond traditional business schools and incubators, with academic libraries playing an increasingly significant role. While accelerators and entrepreneurship centers focus on commercialization, libraries contribute by developing foundational business skills, research expertise, and access to specialized resources by offering different resources. Licensing agreements restrict direct commercial use of many library resources thereby limiting their role to skill development, apart from funding, staffing related issues. Libraries act as knowledge hubs, guiding entrepreneurs toward relevant tools rather than offering direct business advice. However, the existing skill sets of librarians can be highly valuable, and current library services could be further innovated by repositioning existing programs to better support students, researchers, faculty, and alumni aiming to develop their entrepreneurship skills. Additionally, accelerators that focus on bridging academia and practice—by making study curricula more practical through collaborations with external businesses—can help raise awareness of library offerings among students and foster an entrepreneurial mindset. On the contrary, library support could help accelerators leverage existing library resources (subject to licensing agreements), thereby reducing the need for reinvestment in resource procurement.

Entrepreneurs often require more than research support—they need mentorship, funding opportunities, and networking connections that libraries alone cannot provide. This is where accelerators become essential. At the University of Toronto, the entrepreneurship ecosystem consists of 12 accelerators; some of them do offer comprehensive startup support, including coworking spaces, venture mentorship services, and industry connections. Similarly, Harvard University's Baker Library collaborates with Harvard Innovation Labs and the Rock Center for Entrepreneurship to provide student entrepreneurs with business research guidance while directing them to external resources for commercialization. These examples highlight that while academic libraries equip entrepreneurs with knowledge, entrepreneurs require more collaborations, including with externals translate ideas into commercialisation. The entrepreneurship journey should be viewed as a series of stages—from skill development to the actual transition of ideas into market-ready products or services. This progression requires the involvement of multiple actors, including libraries, academic departments, accelerators, and external business support professionals such as mentors and industry practitioners.

Public libraries also play a vital role in supporting entrepreneurs, particularly those outside the university system. The Toronto Public Library, for example, offers databases, business workshops, and consultations with business librarians, making its services accessible to a wider audience, including small business owners. Programs like the Entrepreneur in Residence initiative provide mentorship and personalized feedback on business ideas, helping local entrepreneurs refine their strategies. Public libraries can serve as strategic partners to academic libraries and university accelerators by providing foundational business education and extending resources beyond university-affiliated individuals. Their ability to bridge the gap between academic research and real-world business application makes them valuable contributors to the broader entrepreneurial ecosystem.

The collaboration between academic libraries, public libraries, and university accelerators creates a multi-layered support system for entrepreneurs. Academic libraries lay the groundwork by developing research and analytical skills, public libraries could collaborate in this skills development initiative and could also collaborate with accelerators to leverage the resources to help entrepreneurs to get more customised support, for instance by helping them get mentorship and industry connections from its partners. This interconnected ecosystem ensures that entrepreneurs receive comprehensive support at different stages of their journey, reinforcing the importance of libraries as key stakeholders in entrepreneurship development. However, for libraries to maximize their impact, ongoing partnerships with external organizations, active use of digital engagement tools, and strategic integration into entrepreneurship ecosystems will be essential.

AI Technology Adoption Among Libraries and Entrepreneurs

5

This chapter aims to explore the adoption of artificial intelligence (AI) technologies—particularly Generative AI (GenAI)—by librarians and entrepreneurs, and to examine how they successfully co-experimented to uncover its practical applications. Specifically, it highlights their collaborative efforts in developing a comprehensive handbook for patrons interested in setting up a sole proprietorship, enriched with informative materials and references to relevant external support actors. The case also demonstrates how the process of co-experimentation itself served as a mechanism for strengthening adoption factors—such as social influence, domain experience, and technological familiarity—regardless of whether libraries ultimately decided to integrate the technology long-term. Even in instances where adoption was partial or deferred, these collaborative trials helped participants to identify both valuable use cases and critical misuse risks, thereby building institutional knowledge and capacity for informed decision-making around GenAI technologies.

This chapter also presents a 2024 case study demonstrating how co-experimentation between a mid-sized public library, local entrepreneurs, and the author (as the consultant) positively influenced Generative AI adoption factors by creating a synergistic environment. This collaboration enabled more effective technology experimentation and resulted in the co-creation of business reference materials that combined AI-generated outputs, professional expertise, and research-based facts.

Factors Influencing Generative AI (GenAI) Adoption by Librarians and Entrepreneurs
Gupta (2024b) empirically validated the factors influencing librarians' adoption of Generative AI technologies, particularly ChatGPT, for business support services. It examines

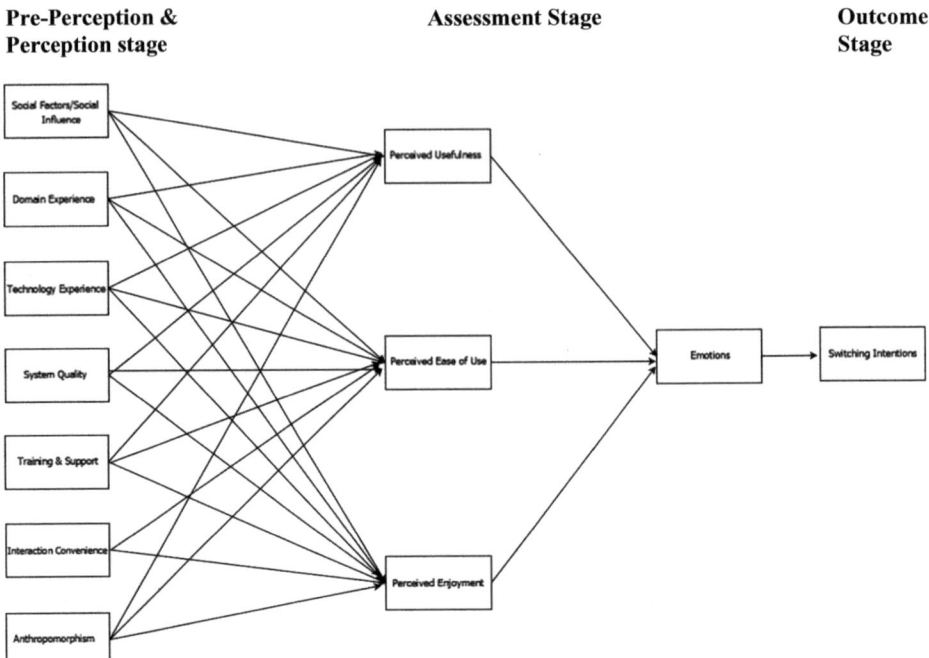

Fig. 5.1 Relationship between adoption factors (Taken from Gupta 2024a and adapted from Gupta and Yang 2024b, Published with license by Taylor & Francis Group, LLC, reprinted with permission of Taylor & Francis Ltd, http://www.tandfonline.com. The figure remains under the standard Taylor & Francis license)

the diverse factors shaping their decision to adopt these technologies or switch to alternative solutions. The relationships between the adoption factors across the three adoption stages is graphically represented by Fig. 5.1.

The research study conducted by Gupta (2024b) has the following results:

- In the continuously innovating technological environment, libraries face challenges in digital transformation to meet patron expectations. Social influence plays a crucial role in making librarians aware of the new technologies in the market and shaping their perceptions about them. Academic libraries support teaching, research, and building entrepreneurship skills of the entrepreneurs, while public libraries cater to diverse patrons beyond universities, including support for entrepreneurs looking for commercialising their ideas (see Chap. 4). Libraries strategically partner with academic departments, research institutions, and external business support actors. Librarians actively engage in discussions on AI integration into education and library services (Gupta 2024c), balancing academic integrity concerns with the need for innovation (Gupta 2024e).

Librarians, regardless of direct business support involvement, contribute to entrepreneurs by providing resources including AI technologies instructional materials (refer to Chap. 8 for reference instructional materials of ASReview, Connected Papers, and Citation Gecko technologies). There are continuous experimentations with AI technologies and discussions within the libraries and with external innovation actors, which occur in formal and informal settings—websites, blogs, Listservs, and in-person exchanges. In these discussions the librarians share experiences, successes, and emerging trends, increasing awareness and fostering curiosity. The patrons and externals are also invited to share their experiences and take part in co-experimentations with AI technologies.

Amid rising patron inquiries about AI (e.g., AI in research), such exchanges encourage libraries to explore these technologies. The initial curiosity and need to serve patrons prompt experimentation with tools like ChatGPT. As experimentation scales, perceptions of usefulness, ease of use, and enjoyment grow. This confirms that social influence positively impacts Perceived Usefulness (PU), Perceived Ease of Use (PEU), and Perceived Enjoyment (PE). This is in line with the findings of previous studies that social influences play an important role in the adoption of technologies, for instance, AI technology among users (Kelly, Kaye, and Oviedo-Trespalacios 2022; Gursoy et al. 2019; Lu et al. 2019; Romero et al. 2023; Emon et al. 2023; Ma and Huo 2023; Khan 2020; Gupta, Guptaet al. 2022).

- Another key finding is that domain expertise positively influences perceived usefulness (PU), perceived ease of use (PEU), and performance expectancy (PE). Librarians who support entrepreneurs often develop business knowledge through formal education or hands-on experience within innovation ecosystems. This expertise enhances their ability to identify practical AI use cases, understand limitations, and assess the business value of technologies like ChatGPT. As a result, domain expertise equips librarians to strategically apply these tools to streamline business processes more effectively.

Gupta (2024) reported two notable examples of ChatGPT experimentation in business support as mentioned by the surveyed participants in response to the survey open ended questions.

- One librarian explores the use of ChatGPT to assist in creating guidelines for conducting surveys to gather customer needs in foreign markets. Drawing upon their expertise in survey design, market research methodologies, and cultural understanding of the foreign country, the librarian assesses the technology's capacity to generate comprehensive and relevant guidelines that align with the unique needs of the business aiming at globalizing in foreign markets.
- Another librarian, drawing from their previous experience assisting businesses in global expansion efforts, decided to replicate the project but this time getting help from ChatGPT alone. Having previously relied on a combination of market data gathered from expert interviews, customer interactions, and Google technologies,

the librarian sought to explore the potential of ChatGPT as a standalone tool for guiding global expansion strategies. Utilizing their domain expertise in business support and market analysis, the librarian posed a series of globalization-related questions to ChatGPT, aiming to glean insights that could inform the team's direction for international expansion. As the interactions with technology grew, librarians strengthened their perceptions about the technology's usefulness, ease of use, and enjoyment, identifying functional capabilities and limitations. Limitations were never a problem, as technology is still evolving, and there are possible use cases where it could help the librarian in his business support efforts.

- Technology quality plays a vital role in shaping librarians' perceptions of ChatGPT's usefulness, ease of use, and overall enjoyment in delivering business support services. Librarians typically begin by experimenting with AI technologies on simple tasks, and as task complexity increases, their confidence and positive perceptions also grow, to meet information needs of the entrepreneurs. Given the wide range of business support services, evaluating AI's effectiveness in knowledge-intensive tasks—such as foreign market analysis—remains a complex challenge. High-quality technology helps overcome librarians' reluctance toward adopting innovations and enhances their ability to meet business needs. Previous research confirms that key service quality attributes—such as functionality, reliability, speed, and accuracy—strongly shape user expectations (Gursoy et al. 2019; Lu et al. 2019).

Gupta (2024) reported one quote shared by the surveyed participants in response to the survey open ended questions. This pertains to the case of one the surveyed librarian about his experiment to explore the capabilities of ChatGPT for gathering information on women's entrepreneurship and relevant references. This experimentation aimed to support faculty members by providing them with introductory content and insights about requested research topics. While the information generated by ChatGPT appeared convincing at first glance, the librarian, an expert in the field, recognized the importance of refining the process for better content quality. The librarian discovered that by using different prompts and validating each response, the generated content could be enhanced. Despite this need for refinement, the technology was perceived as highly useful, easy to use, and enjoyable. In addition, librarians do express the desire to do backward tracing from technology responses to the data sources in the future. This signifies that librarians do recognize the credibility of the data sources as one of the factors re-sponsible for the technology quality. The librarian found it empowering to effortlessly navigate and adapt the generated text, rather than starting from scratch, ultimately enhancing their overall experience with the technology.

- Training and support significantly enhance librarians' perceptions of ChatGPT's usefulness, ease of use, and enjoyment. Well-designed training enables librarians to develop high-quality prompts, resulting in more effective AI outputs, and better understanding of the ethical issues involved in interactions with these technologies. Awareness of ethical issues helps them to follow existing protocols to balance innovations with ethical issues to experiment with technology more confidently. Research indicates that librarians already possess many skills aligned with prompt engineering (Frederick 2023) and that such training can be integrated into broader information literacy initiatives (Lund 2023). This approach leverages their existing motivation to improve information-seeking tasks and reduces the learning curve due to their prior experience in this area. ChatGPT's relatively low training requirements further facilitate adoption, and as librarians continue to use the tool, their skills improve—reinforcing favorable perceptions. These findings align with Duong, Vu, and Ngo (2023), who highlight the positive impact of training on both effort and performance expectancy related to technology use.

As discussed earlier, the training should also address ethical AI use within regulatory frameworks. Librarians must be trained in handling sensitive data responsibly, understanding AI privacy policies, and aligning with legal standards. This aligns with the study by Lund (2023), which suggests that librarians should emphasize ethical issues, policies, and regulations during their prompt engineering training sessions. This approach will help librarians overcome their resistance to experimenting with AI technologies due to concerns about data sensitivity. Equipping them with the necessary knowledge and skills to handle these challenges ethically and legally, fosters a more open environment for experimentation, ultimately leading to the adoption of these technologies or informed decisions about whether to switch to them.

Gupta (2024) also shared response of one of the survey respondents that mentioned how the library began using ChatGPT with simple prompts to generate invitations for an entrepreneur event and found the technology easy to use, useful, and enjoyable. Encouraged by this initial success, the librarian scaled up efforts by tackling more complex tasks and refining prompt design. This improvement was guided by recent re-search papers on prompts in the library context and online tutorials. Although the generated outcomes often required adaptations, the librarian perceived the technology as useful and easy to use and enjoyed the process. It provided clear directions and significantly reduced the effort needed to create content from scratch.

- ChatGPT's intuitive interface encourages librarians to experiment with the technology, enhancing interaction convenience. Its ability to mimic human conversation (anthropomorphism) further boosts engagement and makes interactions more natural. Clear, well-structured responses contribute to positive perceptions of usefulness, even when limitations exist. Together, these features lower resistance and make AI easier and more enjoyable to explore within business support contexts. The influence of anthropomorphism on perceived usefulness, ease of use, and enjoyment aligns with findings from Duong, Vu, and Ngo (2023), Ma and Hua (2023), and Strzelecki (2023).

- Positive and negative experiences shape librarian emotions, influencing technology adoption. Enjoyable interactions encourage AI use, while frustrations can deter adoption. This is in line with findings that users who find interacting with technology enjoyable are more inclined to embrace and utilize it, driven by their positive emotional responses (Mustafa and Wen 2022).

  Gupta (2024) highlighted the views of one of the librarians that librarians (as technology user) develop perceptions of usefulness, ease of use, and enjoyment incrementally, leading to positive emotions over time. Even small experiments are valuable, as each contributes to the librarian's expectations and understanding of the technology. Business support encompasses diverse tasks, ranging from less knowledge-intensive to more knowledge-intensive activities. Less knowledge-intensive tasks often include a significant amount of routine and repetitive work. The support provided by technology like ChatGPT is particularly valuable if it helps librarians achieve their goals with less effort. This incremental development of positive perceptions and emotions enhances librarians' willingness to adopt and utilize the technology in their business support activities.

- Librarians' intentions to switch to using Generative AI technologies appear unaffected by demographic factors such as age, gender, years of business support experience, or educational background. This is likely due to four key reasons. First, academic institutions strongly encourage experimentation with new technologies, involving librarians in interdisciplinary teams and responding to patron demand, which drives rational, stakeholder-led decisions rather than demographic influence. Second, tools like Chat-GPT are designed to be intuitive and widely accessible, encouraging experimentation across demographic lines; however, effective integration into library services still requires time, knowledge, and ongoing trials, making demographics less relevant. Third, the rapid pace of technological change often outpaces librarians' ability to evaluate long-term impacts, prompting continuous adaptation over personal traits. Finally, concerns about privacy and policy also temper adoption, suggesting that reluctance to switch is more about caution than demographics.

Gupta (2024b) empirically validates the Generative AI (GenAI) technology adoption model from the perspective of entrepreneurs and confirms that the adoption factors are the same as those identified for librarians. These include social influence, domain experience, technological familiarity, system quality, training and support, and others—each influencing perceived usefulness, ease of use, enjoyment, and emotions. The study highlights how entrepreneurs, like librarians, experience these factors dynamically and interdependently. For instance, exposure through social networks enhances not just perceived usefulness but also enjoyment and ease of use, prompting initial experimentation.

Entrepreneurs' industry expertise and even basic awareness of GenAI help them align the technology with real business needs, deepening their understanding over time. Familiarity with these technologies encourages experimentation, while system quality and user-friendliness build trust and reinforce continued engagement. Training materials help overcome early challenges and improve prompt quality. As with librarians, entrepreneurs experience growing emotional attachment to the technology as they use it across increasingly complex tasks. Positive emotions accelerate adoption, whereas negative experiences can lead to caution or exploration of alternatives. Notably, demographic factors such as age, gender, and education have limited influence on adoption decisions.

What Makes GenAI Adoption Different from Other Technologies, for Instance Social Networking Sites

The adoption of Social Networking Sites (SNS) and Generative AI (GenAI) by librarians for business support reveals key differences in drivers, challenges, and application depth. SNS adoption is largely influenced by Quality, brand image, perceived usefulness, perceived ease of use, and Behavioral Intention, with librarians leveraging platforms like Facebook and LinkedIn for networking, market research, and community engagement (Gupta et al. 2022). Since these platforms integrate seamlessly with daily digital habits, librarians do not require extensive training to utilize them effectively. Brand image plays a significant role in determining which platforms librarians adopt, favouring well-established platforms like Facebook and LinkedIn over lesser-known alternatives. While previous experience with the technology in job tasks, training and computer self-efficacy have minimal impact on SNS adoption, privacy concerns arise mainly when sharing startup-related information, but beyond this, the platforms themselves pose minimal ethical dilemmas. However, since SNS tools are widely accepted and embedded in everyday communication, librarians do not need extensive experimentation to determine their value—most functionalities are straightforward and require minimal additional skills.

In contrast, GenAI adoption is shaped by social influence, domain expertise, familiarity with technology, system quality, training and support, interaction convenience, anthropomorphism, perceptions of usefulness, ease of use, and enjoyment. These perceptions influence librarians' emotional responses to technology and affect their decisions regarding adoption or considering alternative options. Librarians' engagement with AI tools like ChatGPT is driven by curiosity, interdisciplinary collaboration, and the need to respond to growing patron interest in AI applications. Unlike SNS, where perceived usefulness is inherent due to widespread adoption in personal lives, GenAI requires continuous experimentation for users to fully grasp its capabilities, limitations, and business applications, to develop perceptions about its usefulness, ease of use, and gaining enjoyment with the technology. Privacy and ethical concerns in GenAI are more pronounced, as librarians must carefully assess data-sharing policies, model training sources, and regulatory frameworks to ensure responsible AI use.

Unlike SNS, where the interaction is more like a routine task after several continuous interactions, GenAI requires continuous experimentation to identify effective use cases, particularly as applications range from low-knowledge-intensive tasks (such as content generation) to high-knowledge-intensive tasks (such as foreign market analysis). Technology quality directly affects perceptions of usefulness, ease of use, and enjoyment as high-performing AI tools reduce resistance and improve confidence in their business applications. However, to apply the information obtained from the GenAI, there is a need to evaluate its accuracy, for which training and support mechanisms, domain experience, and familiarity with the technology are more crucial than for SNS. This will help to so effective prompt engineering and enhancing the understanding of AI's evolving nature to extract maximum value from the technology while mitigating its limitations. Interaction convenience, and anthropomorphism fosters the interactions with the technology, together with the other factors, the user develops perceptions about its usefulness, ease of use, enjoyment, leading to adoption of switching decisions.

Synergizing Librarian and Entrepreneur Adoption Drivers to Enable GenAI Experimentation

To foster co-creation and experimentation with GenAI, library managers must create an environment that aligns with these adoption factors *that are common for both librarians and entrepreneurs* to felicitate co-creation driven experimentations with GenAI thereby identifying number of use cases *and misuse cases)* further strengthening curiosity and need based experimentations in libraries. A collaborative ecosystem can be established through interdisciplinary knowledge-sharing forums, AI experimentation spaces, and learning programs with joint involvement of librarians and the entrepreneurs. The Toronto Public Library (Canada) hosted a program titled "Using AI (ChatGPT) for Small Business—Analytics, Marketing, and Assistance" on August 8, 2024. The event featured an external speaker with expertise in both technology and business. The librarian, who also served as the event coordinator, attended the session to gain insights and explore opportunities for future programs or reference instruction on using Generative AI in marketing. Such initiatives foster knowledge sharing and strengthen collaboration between librarians and entrepreneurs, creating opportunities to experiment with emerging technologies and drive innovation together. Given the strong role of social influence in GenAI adoption, library managers should encourage librarians to engage with entrepreneurial networks, industry experts, and AI researchers to exchange insights on AI applications. Co-creation initiatives, such as AI-driven business consultation sessions or AI research partnerships, can enhance mutual learning. By embedding GenAI discussions into library innovation groups, managers can ensure that librarians remain at the forefront of AI adoption and can effectively guide entrepreneurs in leveraging AI for business growth.

Since domain expertise significantly impacts AI adoption, library managers should facilitate professional development programs that strengthen librarians' expertise in business domain, especially business librarians. library managers should support skill development through tailored AI literacy programs and business-oriented training sessions-inhouse programs, external programs, like those by Harvard, LinkedIn, Coursera, or incubators. Business librarians and entrepreneurs can co-create to transfer their domain skills leading to better experimentations with AI and identification of more use cases. Familiarity with GenAI can thus further be enhanced by encouraging hands-on interaction with AI tools in a low-risk environment, in collaboration with entrepreneurs, taking real business scenarios possible experimentation use cases where librarians can explore its capabilities without pressure.

To support ongoing experimentation, library managers should provide structured yet flexible training in AI literacy, prompt engineering, and ethical AI use. Unlike SNS, where librarians can rely on intuitive functionality, GenAI requires adaptive learning processes. Providing access to AI tools, workshops, and sandbox environments where librarians and entrepreneurs can experiment with AI applications will enhance their engagement. AI training should emphasize iterative learning, allowing users to refine their approach over time rather than expecting immediate proficiency.

Privacy and technology governance frameworks should be integrated into AI experimentation efforts to address concerns about data sharing, content reliability, and compliance (*need for AI experimentation policy*). Managers can implement ethical AI guidelines, establish protocols for validating AI-generated information, and ensure that AI adoption aligns with institutional policies. This will help reduce librarian resistance to AI experimentation while ensuring responsible AI use. This will help librarians to boost their technology experimentations in collaboration with the entrepreneurs. This is made possible by overcoming their concerns, particularly regarding ethical issues such as privacy which other wise inhibit their motivation to conduct experimentations as reported by Lo (2024) and Kaushal and Yadav (2022).

Finally, managers should foster a culture of innovation by promoting a mindset of incremental experimentation, with each experimentation outcome evaluated and reported *(M&E of AI experimentations)* encouraging librarians and entrepreneurs to test AI applications in small, scalable ways before making full-scale adoption decisions. Recognizing and showcasing successful AI-driven projects can further reinforce positive perceptions of AI's usefulness, ease of use, and enjoyment. By structuring an ecosystem where collaboration, continuous learning, and ethical AI experimentation are prioritized, library managers can ensure that librarians and entrepreneurs harness the full potential of GenAI for business support while navigating its challenges effectively.

Case Study: Co-creating Business Reference Materials with ChatGPT: A Library-Entrepreneurial Success Story

In early 2024, a mid-sized public library that was offering business support services, embarked on an innovative journey to adopt Generative AI (GenAI)—specifically, Chat-GPT—to enhance its role as a business knowledge hub. This initiative emerged as part of the library's broader strategy to foster digital transformation and strengthen ties with local entrepreneurs. This case was notably supported through consulting by the author, who collaborated with the library team to explore GenAI technologies in the context of reference services for entrepreneurs. Some local entrepreneurs were also invited to explore these emerging technologies together with the librarians to leverage their expertise in business domains and GenAI. One of objective of experimenting with GenAI with the entrepreneurs is to seek their support in co-developing dynamic business reference guides for early-stage entrepreneurs—covering essential topics like taxation, marketing, research tools, and business models.

It is important to note that the stages presented in this case did not unfold in a strictly linear fashion. Instead, the journey of adopting ChatGPT was characterized by ongoing co-experimentations, each triggered and shaped by the evolving levels of adoption factors. These factors—such as social influence, domain experience, technological familiarity, system quality, and training support—were not confined to isolated phases. Rather, there was a continuous interplay between factors in the Pre-Perception and Perception Phase and those in the Assessment Phase. At each stage, a baseline level of adoption factors existed, but as co-experimentation progressed—through joint activities like prompt refinement or tax related document analysis—certain factors were enhanced, which in turn amplified others. This dynamic interaction allowed librarians and entrepreneurs to iteratively refine their use of the technology, better identify use and misuse cases, and integrate AI-generated outputs more meaningfully with human expertise and research-based knowledge. As a result, the overall process became a cumulative and reinforcing cycle, where each phase of experimentation contributed to deeper learning, emotional engagement, and ultimately, the decision to adopt ChatGPT as a core tool in the library's entrepreneurial support services.

Stage 1: Awareness and Social Influence

The project was sparked during a library-hosted innovation day, where local entrepreneurs demonstrated how they had used ChatGPT to generate market entry strategies and identify regulatory hurdles. Further, the interactions between some entrepreneurs and reference librarians during one-to-one consultations also fostered the awareness and interests to further explore this technology possible use cases for the library. This real-world application caught the attention of librarians, who had previously viewed the tool primarily as a novelty for basic queries.

"We didn't realize it could go beyond writing paragraphs—seeing it used to break down business challenges made us rethink its potential", shared one business reference librarian.

This social influence, a key factor in the Pre-Perception and Perception Phase, triggered curiosity and initial discussions. It created early motivation to explore how ChatGPT could extend the library's existing role in supporting entrepreneurs.

Stage 2: Initial Experimentation—Leveraging Domain Synergy together with other adoption factors

The library's business support team and local entrepreneurs began co-working on trial prompts to answer practical questions like:

> What are the steps to register as a sole proprietor in Spain?

> How can I validate a startup idea using free tools and which accelerators or business support actors are available in Spain?

This stage leveraged domain experience on both sides: librarians contributed experience from years of business literacy training, while entrepreneurs brought real-world problems and local context. For example, librarians initially asked ChatGPT:

> Explain the difference between sole proprietorship and LLC.

Entrepreneurs refined this to:

> Compare tax liabilities and liability exposure for sole proprietorship vs. LLC (Sociedad de Responsabilidad Limitada (S.L.)) in Spain, with examples for digital businesses under €50K revenue.

This prompt refinement improved output quality. The domain experience helped to narrow down the prompts, and validate the AI output, strengthening technological familiarity and understanding of the System Quality. The sessions also exposed gaps—ChatGPT sometimes produced oversimplified or generic content, prompting users to iterate and verify outputs in iterative and incremental manner.

Stage 3: Technological Familiarity Enables Deeper Engagement

As experimentations progressed, librarians grew more comfortable navigating ChatGPT's capabilities. Simple interactions evolved into more complex tasks, such as:

(a) Structuring entire business support workshop focusing on setting businesses for buddy entrepreneur training sessions, including reference materials,
(b) Drafting comparative analyses of free marketing tools, including market research tools, and
(c) Customizing business setting and tax related instruction materials aligning with the recent regulations in place.

The increase in technological familiarity directly boosted perceived ease of use (PEU). One librarian quoted, *"At first, we didn't know how to frame questions. Now we're experimenting with multi-step prompts that combine context, tone, and format together with the real facts drawn from our experiences and through research of public documents"*. This growing competence allowed librarians to transition from passive users to active co-designers of content—increasing their perceived usefulness (PU) and enjoyment (PE) with each iteration.

Stage 4: System Quality, professional experiences and deeper research—Collaborative Refinement

Fuelled with the enhanced levels of the adoption factors at Pre-Perception and Perception as well as assessment phase, librarians and entrepreneurs began uploading longer publicly available documents—legal PDFs, policy briefs, and grant guidelines—into ChatGPT (enterprise version), testing its ability to extract structured summaries and key insights from the document. For instance, one tax related 40-page reference material was uploaded and summarized by ChatGPT. The result included useful sections but also misinterpreted key thresholds. Instead of discarding the output, the team worked together to use AI for initial structuring, validate legal accuracy together, and refine the information by adding the information that are grounded on their tax related professional experiences, and those drawn from studying the current regulation in place. This co-review process reinforced trust in the system's capabilities, while acknowledging its limits. It directly improved perceptions of system quality (SQ) and solidified librarians' understanding of misuse risks—thus enhancing their ability to teach responsible AI use to patrons. One of the business reference librarians quoted, *"We treat it like a research assistant, not a legal expert. But it saves us hours of work* as it's much easier to refine the technology output rather writing everything from scratch".

Stage 5: Co-training as a Catalyst—Further Reinforcing and Expanding Adoption Factors

One of the most powerful moments came during a prompt engineering workshop co-hosted by the library and entrepreneurs. As the participants co-developed prompt libraries, individual adoption factors began reinforcing each other further. Training and Support (TS) activities directly improved Technological Familiarity (TF) and better prompts revealed more nuanced capabilities, increasing System Quality (SQ) perception. The ability to collaboratively adapt prompts to specific tasks improved Domain Experience (DE) and prompted further experimentation. For instance, during a session on marketing strategies, a librarian asked ChatGPT:

List free digital marketing tools

An entrepreneur revised it:

List free AI-powered marketing tools for early-stage Spanish startups in B2C sectors

The enhanced output was so context-specific and rich that the team added it to their official business startup guide, a product of their co-experimentation. This kind of interactive training, driven by mutual learning, proved more effective than static tutorials. As one librarian noted, *"Learning with entrepreneurs helps us build the resource and the skillset simultaneously"*. All these factors influenced each other, and all together impacted the emotions towards the technology. The positive emotions (excitement, pride, empowerment) generated by this journey had a direct impact on the final adoption decision. The tool was no longer seen as a tech curiosity—it had become a strategic extension of the library's value proposition at least for creating the reference materials for the patrons looking for starting their business. *"We're not replacing what we do—we're amplifying it at least leveraging strengths of the technology and identifying others based on its limitations"*, concluded one team member. The enhanced experience with successive experimentations triggers another round of successive experimentations to further identify the possible use cases of the technology. Finally, after successive experimentations, the handbook for patrons looking for setting up the business-sole proprietorship was created with informative materials and references to external support actors.

This suggests that factors in the Pre-perception and Perception Phase function not only independently but also interdependently—where the strength of one factor can initiate or enhance experimentation, which in turn stimulates growth in other factors. The initial levels of adoption factors—such as social influence, domain experience, or technological familiarity—can drive early-stage experimentation with Generative AI technologies. However, as librarians and entrepreneurs continue to co-experiment, these factors begin to evolve and strengthen through practice. For example, engaging in specialized joint training, such as prompt engineering workshops, not only deepens technological familiarity but also enhances domain understanding, and perceived system quality.

This iterative process creates a reinforcing loop, where improvements in one factor begin to boost others, leading to more sophisticated experimentation and a sharper ability to identify both the use and misuse cases of the technology. As a result, perceptions of usefulness (PU), ease of use (PEU), and enjoyment (PE) continue to alter, shaping emotional responses (positive, negative or neutral) and ultimately influencing the decision to adopt or integrate the technology into library services. Thus, the co-experimentation process is both dynamic and reinforcing, enabling refinement of existing use cases and contributing to a more robust and sustained integration of Generative AI into library services.

Co-creation and Experimentation to Foster AI Technology Adoption

6

This chapter presents co-creation and structured experimentation as foundational strategies for fostering AI adoption in library-based business support services. This chapter presents a case study of the University of Toronto (UofT) Libraries, focusing on how they are experimenting with AI technologies through incremental, small-scale, and strategic initiatives. It introduces two complementary experimentation frameworks—need-based and curiosity-driven—and explores the synergies between them in practical library contexts. Drawing on real consulting projects, the chapter details how librarians applied the curiosity-based experimentation (CBE) approach to assess a video-to-text AI tool, formulate a business case, and provide evidence-based recommendations for adoption.

It further examines a collaborative experimentation project involving a public library, a university library, and highly engaged users—identified using the Enhanced Business Value Calculator—to explore the use of ChatGPT for systematic literature reviews. Additionally, the chapter reflects on the University of Toronto Libraries' ongoing AI experimentation culture, highlighting their focus on experimenting with AI technologies for their possible adoptions in the libraries. Altogether, the chapter provides a grounded pathway for libraries to integrate AI technologies through co-creation, continuous experimentations, and knowledge sharing's with the peers.

AI Experimentations at University of Toronto (UofT) Libraries
Gupta (2024c) through the case study the University of Toronto (UofT) libraries explore the AI adoption strategy at the UofT libraries, focusing on incremental, small-scale, and strategic experimentation. The results are based on insights shared by the director of strategic initiatives at UofT, and Associate Chief Librarian for Science Research and Information. The findings indicate that UofT libraries adopt AI through a hybrid model,

V. Gupta, *Libraries as Hubs for Entrepreneurship*, Synthesis Lectures on Information Concepts, Retrieval, and Services, https://doi.org/10.1007/978-3-032-03569-1_6

balancing top-down leadership-driven initiatives with bottom-up experimentation by individual librarians. Discussions on AI are a regular part of the UofT Library Executive Council's weekly meetings, and an annual retreat allows for in-depth conversations on the topic. This reflects a strategic, incremental adoption of AI, ensuring resources are not committed all at once without clear value. This approach "avoids the situation where they are devoting all resources in a 'one-go' fashion without fully knowing their potential and the areas in which they could create significant value."

The weekly newsletter, In the Loop, plays a key role in AI awareness, featuring a nine-week Special Series: Artificial Intelligence that introduces various AI tools. This newsletter communicates some of the AI tools to inform librarians about these tools that they can experiment with. The outcomes of these experiments then could be shared with peers which could ultimately lead to its adoption in the library. For example, the March 29, 2023, edition highlighted Scholarcy, an AI tool that "summarizes articles and creates and transforms lengthy articles into summaries in the form of interactive flashcards". Scholarcy's deep learning technology breaks down complex scholarly texts into digestible sections, including key findings and links to open-access sources.

UofT Libraries also encourage individual libraries (among its 40) to experiment with AI tools on a small scale, sharing successful implementations with peers. This collaborative approach helps the peers to leverage experimentation experiences to further experiment with these technologies fostering informed adoption. According to the Associate Chief Librarian for Science Research and Information, *"One example was around a library collection app (this was a few years ago) that one library had used to help with collection maintenance. This was shared at an internal conference and several libraries were intrigued and also began using the same technology in their spaces"*.

To further engage staff, UofT has incorporated AI exploration into work plans, forming short-term AI working groups. The Associate Chief Librarian noted, *"I have recently formed 4 small AI working groups of short duration to get people discussing and playing with different AI concepts, which will then be shared back to the system writ large"*. Overall, UofT Libraries' approach ensures AI adoption is evidence-driven, encouraging librarians to explore, share, and rationally integrate AI tools that add value while avoiding premature, overhyped adoption.

The research presents a reasoned prediction about the potential impact of AI experimentation on entrepreneurial services at UofT libraries. As discussed in previous chapter, UofT libraries' acts as hubs of entrepreneurship by offering opportunities for entrepreneurial skills development through resources like workshops, training, research tools, makerspace, and networking. The buddy entrepreneurs can then seek more specialised support for commercialisation from some of the accelerators of the University as libraries don't directly support the commercialisation initiatives. The article suggests that AI experimentation plays a role in shaping the entrepreneurs support services. As integral parts of the UofT ecosystem, libraries need to continuously innovate their services especially by digitally transforming using AI technologies.

The culture of AI experimentation within libraries has a positive impact on student entrepreneurs. Libraries support this by offering AI-related training, workshops, educational materials, and guidelines aimed at raising awareness, encouraging hands-on experimentation, promoting ethical and responsible use of technology, and enabling the practical application of AI tools. Conversely, entrepreneurs contribute to this ecosystem by sharing their experiences with emerging AI technologies, providing valuable feedback on tools under experimentation or already implemented in libraries, and actively participating in collaboration, knowledge sharing, and networking efforts. Their insights help shape and refine library services, fostering a reciprocal relationship that advances both entrepreneurial development and library innovation. This underscores the importance of co-creation, where librarians and patrons work together to experiment with the technologies and innovate library services.

Future research should prioritize refining experiment design, with a particular focus on experimentation policies, monitoring and evaluation practices, and fostering stronger collaboration with patrons. Additionally, investigating the factors influencing AI adoption at both organizational and individual levels is crucial for creating a supportive environment for these initiatives. Ongoing AI experiments will enable librarians to critically assess emerging technologies by drawing from hands-on experience with various applications. This approach will help them differentiate practical solutions from market hype, ensuring they focus on innovations that genuinely enhance library operations.

Need-Based and Curiosity-Based Experimentation Frameworks: Exploring Synergies and Practical Implementation in Libraries

Gupta and Gupta (2023a) explores how libraries can integrate artificial intelligence (AI) by leveraging structured experimentation-driven frameworks. The authors introduce two primary approaches: the Need-Based Experimentation (NBE) Framework and the Curiosity-Based Experimentation (CBE) Framework. The NBE Framework is designed to address specific operational challenges within libraries by testing AI solutions that directly meet existing needs. NBE framework, suggest that need driven experimentation process begins by identifying functional pain points, followed by exploring suitable AI tools that could offer practical solutions. Librarians assess internal capacities and define short-term performance indicators to guide experimentation. Through structured small-scale trials, results are analysed and compared, and informed recommendations are made for potential adoption based on the technology's ability to meet operational goals. Figure 6.1 captures the need driven experimentation process (NBE framework).

In contrast, the CBE Framework encourages librarians to explore AI technologies out of curiosity, allowing for innovation and potential future applications. These experimentations then could provide solutions for existing business problems or those that may emerge in near future. In other words, within the CBE context, AI technology experimentation is often driven by librarians' personal curiosity rather than by an intent to address specific library challenges. For example, a librarian might explore a new technology simply to

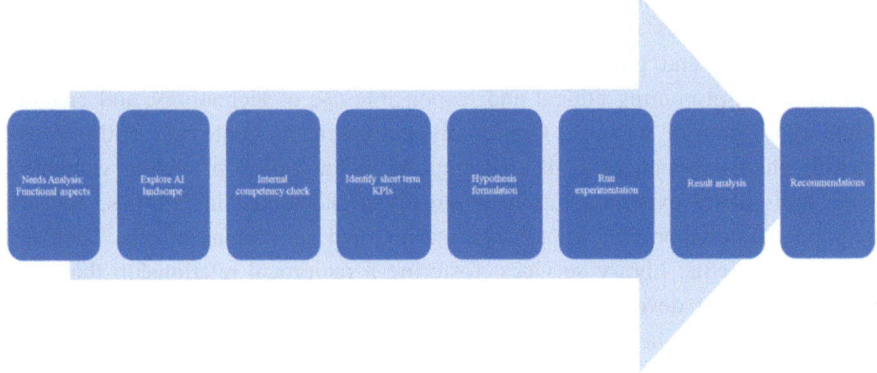

Fig. 6.1 Need driven experimentation process (NBE framework) (Gupta and Gupta 2023a) (© 2023 The authors, reprinted by permission of Taylor & Francis Ltd., http://www.tandfonline.com)

understand how it works or to see how it might assist with their current job tasks. This means that Curiosity-Based Experimentation (CBE) is driven by interest, exploration, or the desire to learn, even in the absence of an immediate problem to solve. A librarian might experiment with an AI tool simply to understand its functionality or to explore how it might be applied to certain library tasks, even if there is no current need for such a solution. In curiosity driven experimentation process (CBE framework) experimentation is driven by enthusiasm for learning and testing new tools. While key performance indicators and hypotheses are still formulated, they may not be directly tied to current library tasks. The focus is on accumulating hands-on experience, generating insights, and documenting possible future applications. Outcomes are compiled into business cases to inform strategic discussions and long-term innovation planning. Figure 6.2 captures the curiosity driven experimentation process (CBE framework).

The study then identified the challenges to AI adoption based on the empirical observations from ten university libraries that are actively undertaking the experimentations. The results indicate that AI adoption in libraries faces multiple challenges such as Financial and Infrastructural, Resistance to change, Awareness and willingness to adopt AI, Skills and Competencies, technology maturity and reliability, Security and intrusion concerns, Lack of exposure to international standards.

Surveyed librarians believe that the proposed framework will address most barriers to AI adoption, based on their experiences with experimentation. Key factors supporting this belief include increased awareness of AI, enhanced user-friendliness of AI technologies, improved perceptions of their usefulness and usability, expanded opportunities for knowledge sharing with peers and external networks, and the development of essential soft skills, such as problem-solving. Open collaboration is crucial for overcoming these challenges and fostering AI experimentation—whether driven by necessity, curiosity, or both. The study concludes that a balanced approach combining both NBE and CBE frameworks

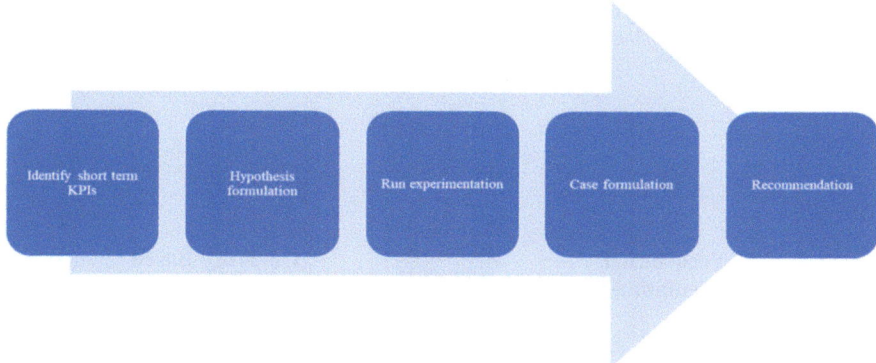

Fig. 6.2 Curiosity driven experimentation process (CBE framework) (Gupta and Gupta 2023a) (© 2023 The authors, reprinted by permission of Taylor & Francis Ltd., http://www.tandfonline.com)

can drive technological transformation in libraries, fostering innovation while addressing real operational needs.

Gupta and Gupta (2023b) expands on the relationship between the two experimentation-driven frameworks, emphasizing their complementary nature. The NBE Framework provides a structured approach for solving immediate problems in libraries, ensuring that AI adoption is purposeful and aligned with institutional goals. Meanwhile, the CBE Framework nurtures a culture of continuous learning, encouraging librarians to explore AI beyond specific needs, leading to unexpected yet valuable applications.

The article argues that by integrating both frameworks, libraries can create an ecosystem where structured AI adoption is enhanced by curiosity-driven exploration (Fig. 6.3). The collaboration between librarians who follow NBE and those who engage in CBE fosters a more dynamic problem-solving environment. When librarians experimenting with AI for finding solutions for the business problems (NBE) interact with those who explore AI out of curiosity (CBE), they can bridge knowledge gaps and identify novel applications for AI technologies. With the participation of librarians that have already tested the technologies driven by their curiosities of in past projects, peer librarians overcome their initial hesitation and find solutions. Successful experiments driven by library needs further secure management's support for curiosity-driven initiatives.

Additionally, librarians exploring AI through CBE acquire valuable technical skills that contribute to library advancements. Their experimentation experiences help address priority library challenges within the NBE framework, fostering a culture of experimentation. NBE bridges CBE with practical library outcomes, ensuring that curiosity-driven exploration translates into impactful, need-driven solutions.

The article also highlights the importance of management support in sustaining this experimentation culture. It recommends allocating time for AI exploration, creating diverse teams, and incentivizing successful AI-driven projects. The culture should

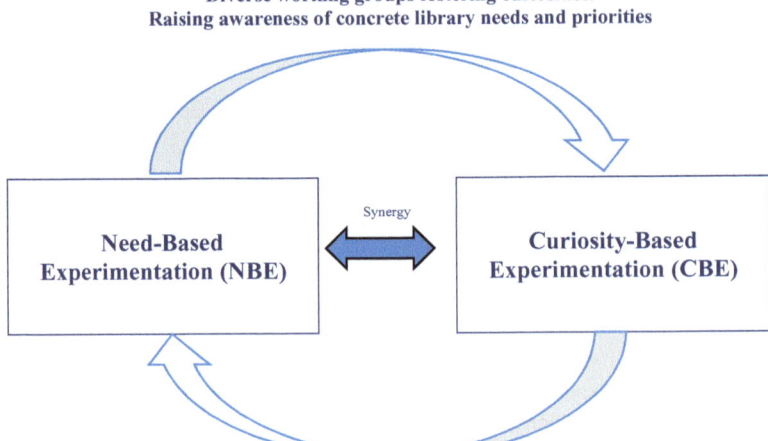

Fig. 6.3 Synergy between NBE and CBE (Gupta and Gupta 2023b) (Copyright © 2023, Emerald Publishing Limited, reprinted by permission of Emerald Publishing Limited, https://www.emerald.com/)

embrace failure and encourage the sharing of experimentation outcomes with peers, regardless of whether the technology proved valuable or not. The conclusion underscores that the synergy between structured and curiosity-driven AI adoption can accelerate the transformation of libraries, making them more adaptable to emerging technologies while simultaneously solving immediate challenges.

Gupta and Gupta (2023c) presents a real-world case study demonstrating how the Curiosity-Based Experimentation (CBE) Framework can be successfully implemented in a library setting. The study follows a librarian who, driven by curiosity, experimented with AI-driven text-to-video generation tools to enhance the library's social media presence and user engagement. Initially, the librarian explored different AI text-to-video generation technologies in the personal life and these experimentations led to an important realization: these AI tools could be leveraged to improve the library's engagement with students, faculty, and entrepreneurs by producing interactive video content (*application of these technologies in library settings*).

Motivated by this insight, the librarian applied the AI-generated text to video technology to the library's social media strategy, creating short, engaging videos of the entrepreneurship events, as the part of the experimentation process. Over a month-long experimentation period, these AI-generated videos were used to promote four entrepreneurship-focused events hosted by the library, featuring external entrepreneurs as well as the librarian himself. Since the videos featured real individuals—library staff and invited entrepreneurs—this experiment was designed in a way that the key ethical issues are considered, i.e., it was ensured that no individual's identity (avatars representing the person featured in the video), or personal story was used without permission. Before creating the videos, the librarian obtained informed consent from the entrepreneurs, including a declaration that all content provided was either their original creation or had been granted appropriate permissions for public use. Furthermore, the invited entrepreneur provided consent for the use of his own avatar in the video, instead of using randomly generated avatars that do not represent any real person. This step was essential to comply with internal data protection policies and external copyright laws.

A key hypothesis for the experimentation was formulated as, *"The videos will increase user engagement on the library website as measured through user likes, dislikes, and shares by at least 40%"*. To measure impact, short-term Key Performance Indicators (KPIs) were established, including average time spent on the website per shared video and the number of likes, dislikes, and shares compared to the previous period. During the experimentation period, the KPIs need to be continuously monitored and analysed to evaluate the success of the experimentation.

The results demonstrated significant improvements in user engagement. The AI-generated videos led to an increase in likes, shares, and overall interaction with the library's social media content. Patrons responded positively, spending more time on the library's digital platforms, particularly those sections related to entrepreneurship support. The presence of well-known experts in AI-generated avatars further contributed to audience interest, resulting in word-of-mouth promotion and greater awareness of the library's initiatives. This outcome highlighted the potential of AI tools to enhance library services, making them more interactive, accessible, and engaging for digital audiences.

The librarian involved in the experimentation provided valuable insights, emphasizing that AI technologies offer numerous practical applications in libraries, provided they are tested through small-scale, controlled experiments. This approach allows libraries to gauge the effectiveness of AI before full-scale implementation. The success of this trial also encouraged greater support from library management for AI-driven projects. The librarian noted that experimentation plays a crucial role in overcoming skepticism and building confidence in AI adoption within library staff, ensuring that technological integration is based on real-world results rather than assumptions or hype.

The business case was formulated by the librarian, with support from the researcher acting as a consultant. The corresponding recommendations are summarized in Table 6.1.

The business case used was a free-form template, allowing the librarian to narrate the experimentation journey, report outcomes, and reflect on where this or similar technologies could be further applied or tested. This format works well for knowledge exchange and quick dissemination of lessons learned. However, to align with the library's monitoring and evaluation (M&E) priorities, there is a growing need for a more structured and advanced experimentation outcome reporting template (as outlined in Chap. 7, Table 7.4

Table 6.1 Business case and recommendations

Business Case: Using AI-Generated Videos to Boost Library Engagement using AI text-to-video tools

---

Why I Started This Experiment

This journey started not with a problem—but with a spark of curiosity. While exploring new AI tools in my personal time, I came across platforms that transform written text into short, animated videos using avatars, voiceovers, and visuals. I found myself fascinated. I played with a few tools, tried different prompts, and produced some surprisingly engaging clips—all just for fun. Then I thought:

"Could we use something like this in our library? Would students or entrepreneurs engage more with our content if it was shared as short videos instead of static text?"

There was no formal need, just an idea—an idea worth exploring. That's when I decided to run a small, low-risk experiment using the Curiosity-Based Experimentation (CBE) Framework

Experiment Design: From Curiosity to Practice

I chose to apply the technology to one of our most active programs: our entrepreneurship support events. Over a four-week period, I created short AI-generated videos (each under 90s) to promote four different events. Each video used AI avatars, including those of external business experts (after taking their consent), and voiceovers to make announcements lively and accessible. I formulated this hypothesis:

"The videos will increase user engagement on our social media and website by at least 40% compared to previous event promotions."

To test this, I defined the following Key Performance Indicators (KPIs):

– Number of Likes, Shares, and Comments on social media posts
– Average Time Spent on the event webpage

What We Learned: Results of the Experiment

After the month-long trial, the data was clear—and exciting:

– Average likes per post increased by 63%
– Shares per post grew by 78%
– Comments per post rose by 75%
– Average time spent on the event webpage more than doubled (from 42 s to 1 min 36 s)

In addition to the numbers, several patrons and partners mentioned the videos in conversations—some even shared their links in external groups like WhatsApp and Instagram. Peer librarians expressed interest in using similar tools, showing that the experiment not only increased user engagement but also sparked broader curiosity and collaboration

What I Learned

This experience taught me that:

– Curiosity is a great starting point. It doesn't take a big budget to try something new
– Starting with personal curiosity removed the pressure to perform or prove—it made space to explore
– The CBE Framework helped structure my idea into a safe, measurable trial—small in scope but rich in insight
– AI tools can make our library services more engaging and visible—but they need to be tested first in a controlled, thoughtful way
– Skepticism can be overcome through real results. My colleagues were cautious at first, but the outcomes changed the conversation. Now they're open to experimenting, too
– Experiment was supported by the library's AI experimentation policy; no personal or sensitive data used, with consent obtained from individuals featured as AI avatars

---

(continued)

Table 6.1 (continued)

Recommendations (for scaling the experimentations and adoption)

Based on this successful trial, I recommend the following steps for our library and others:

- **Integrate AI-Generated Videos into Library Communications with patrons**. This means to make short, visual content part of how we meet patrons *where they are*—especially on mobile and social platforms. This could involve the following:
  - Promoting library upcoming events
  - Highlighting services or new resources
  - Sharing library services impact evaluation results
  - Creating quick guides for new students as this will motivate them to give a deeper read to written materials and seek reference librarian support in person
  - Reference instructions as short videos
- **Expand CBE-Led AI Experimentation Across Other technologies**. Based on successful experimentation, I propose that librarians should also give a try to different technologies available to achieve the following:
  - AI Text-to-Speech (TTS) Generators
  - AI Video Summarization Tools
  - AI Image Generation from Text (Text-to-Image)
  - AI Animation from Text or Script
  - AI Subtitling and Captioning Tools

These tools help serve diverse patrons, especially non-native English speakers who need extra support. Libraries can offer customized services that promote equality, diversity, and inclusivity

As the culture of experimentation grows, to foster it further, I propose we cultivate a practice that after every experimentation, we:

- Publish short blog posts to share experimentation outcomes with the community
- Creating the Reference guides about technologies that are successfully experimented
- Encourage documentation using short CBE case templates. These templates (as the one I am sharing) could be made available internally for peers to learn from outcomes
- There is a need for specialised template for recording the experimentation outcomes to align with the library M&E activities

for this case). While both formats have their value, the free-form template is best suited for quick dissemination of experimentation outcomes for getting quicker feedback from the peers, whereas the structured version reports experimentation in more systematic and professional manner.

In other words, the business case serves as a more generic, accessible format that translates the experimentation into a narrative that's easy to understand for a wider audience—including peers, stakeholders, and non-technical decision-makers. It complements the structured outcome reporting template, which is more technical and designed for library managers, evaluators, and strategic planning. This dual approach ensures that experimentation is both accountable and communicable, supporting a culture of innovation and learning at all levels of the library.

Beyond the immediate results as reported in the study, it highlights several key implications for libraries interested in fostering an experimentation-driven culture. First, libraries should allocate dedicated resources—both in terms of time and funding—for AI experimentation. Experimentation should not be seen as a distraction from core responsibilities but rather as an investment in future innovations. Second, failures should be accepted as part of the learning process, with unsuccessful trials providing valuable lessons for refining future AI adoption strategies. Third, open communication among librarians and other stakeholders is essential for knowledge-sharing, collaboration, and sustained innovation. Establishing documentation practices for AI trials ensures that insights are retained and can inform subsequent projects.

Applying the Enhanced Business Value Calculator: Collaborative Experimentation with Libraries and Patrons
Gupta (2024d) focusses on the practical application of the enhanced Business Value Calculator, an improved version of the Urban Libraries Council's original Business Value Calculator. The tool helps libraries communicate the economic value of their services to patrons and stakeholders by estimating the money users save through library offerings—costs they would otherwise bear independently. Beyond this, the enhanced tool enables libraries to analyse patron service usage patterns, for instance which resources are used a lot and who are the most active users, providing valuable insights to guide strategic decision-making and improve future services. The Enhanced Business Value Calculator, which provides a more detailed categorization of library services and assesses their economic value based on usage data (Gupta, 2023b). This tool helps libraries identify their most engaged users, who can then be invited to participate in co-creation efforts aimed at refining services and experimenting with new technologies. By involving these high-performing users, libraries create a continuous cycle of feedback and innovation that enhances their offerings. This tool helps libraries systematically organize and evaluate the services they offer. It uses a structured, tiered approach: broad service categories are broken down into more specific sub-services. The model is flexible, allowing each library to tailor the framework based on its own offerings. The possible structure with 5 service categories is shown below (Table 6.2).

Libraries can track how often each service (or sub-service) is used and assign a value to that usage. By multiplying usage frequency for all the users with assigned service (or sub-service) rates and summing the totals, they can estimate the overall economic value their services deliver.

A case study demonstrates how this tool was applied in a collaborative experiment between a public library and a university library. The experiment involved offering "ChatGPT for systematic literature reviews" service of the library. The service offers comprehensive instructions on how to utilize it ethically and for different types of entrepreneurship activities Over a one-month trial period, libraries identified 270 entrepreneurs (120 from academia and 150 from public library members) who actively used the service. The experiment then involved selecting users who were already utilizing library services for business research and entrepreneurship. These patrons were

Table 6.2 Enhanced business value calculator framework (Gupta 2023b) (Copyright © 2023 The Authors, reprinted by permission of Taylor & Francis Ltd., http://www.tandfonline.com)

Services (and sub-services)	Meaning of the service	Usage rate for all users for each subcategory	Cost per single use

• **Technology Services**
  – Online Databases
  – AI-Driven applications
    Application 1
    Application 2
  – Prototyping technologies
    Prototyping technology 1
    Prototyping technology 2
  – Video production technology
    Video production technology 1
    Video production technology 2
  – Other technologies offered
	The library provides a range of technology solutions and helps under this broad area		

• **Reading Services**
  – Books:
    Book 1
    Book 2
    Book 3
  – Magazines
    Magazine 1
    Magazine 2
  – Research articles
    Research article 1
    Research article 2
  – Other material
	Traditional library services pertaining to reading materials (both online and print) fall under this main category		

(continued)

Table 6.2 (continued)

Services (and sub-services)	Meaning of the service	Usage rate for all users for each subcategory	Cost per single use

• **Consultation Services**
  – Business advisory services
    Service 1
    Service 2
  – Industry-specific consultations
    Service 1
    Service 2
  – Bibliographic literature consultations
    Service 1
    Service 2
  – Other consultations:
	The library offers expert advice and consultations (including through third parties) under this heading		

• **Training Programs**
  – Entrepreneurial Workshops
    Service 1
    Service 2
  – Skill development seminars
    Service 1
    Service 2
  – Entrepreneur-in residence
    Service 1
    Service 2
  – Learning programs (for instance, university courses)
    Service 1
    Service 2
  – Incubator/Accelerator programs
    Service 1
    Service 2
  – Other trainings
	Library training programs offer hands-on workshops, skill-building seminars, and entrepreneurship support to help them build entrepreneurship skills. These programs could be offered by librarians or by external business support actors		

• **Collaborative Spaces and other usage**
    Service 1
    Service 2
	• This highlights the charges for using library space for reading or business meetings as well as use of computer, printers, scanners, etc.		

then engaged in structured experimentations where they provided feedback on ChatGPT-generated content by identifying and using the other information sources, helped in designing prompts, identified technology limitations, and suggested improvements. The findings revealed that while ChatGPT could significantly enhance research efficiency, it also presented challenges such as misinformation, fabricated citations, and a lack of contextual accuracy. As a result, the libraries decided on a partial adoption strategy, where ChatGPT would be used as a supplementary tool rather than a primary resource for literature reviews. This incremental adoption approach allows libraries to build expertise in AI tools while mitigating potential risks.

The study underscores the broader implications of co-creation and experimentation in libraries, emphasizing that involving users in technology adoption leads to more effective and sustainable innovations. It also highlights how public libraries can strengthen their partnerships with external stakeholders, including universities, academic libraries, and industry experts, to provide comprehensive business support. The Enhanced Business Value Calculator plays a crucial role in this ecosystem by identifying service gaps, actors suitable for co-creation, and ensuring that technology investments align stems from real experiences with it rather through market hypes.

This chapter indicate that AI adoption in libraries is most effective when guided by structured, iterative experimentation rather than immediate large-scale implementation. Libraries that follow a dual experimentation model—Need-Based Experimentation (NBE) and Curiosity-Based Experimentation (CBE)—achieve better outcomes by ensuring AI adoption aligns with both immediate operational needs and long-term innovation strategies. Additionally, AI-driven decision-making through tools like the Enhanced Business Value Calculator optimizes technology investments and service improvements. By leveraging data insights on user engagement and service impact, libraries can make more informed decisions regarding which AI technologies to adopt, modify, or phase out. Furthermore, patron co-creation is a critical driver of AI adoption success. Libraries that actively involve users in AI experiments gain valuable real-world feedback, enhance patron engagement, and develop AI-powered services that meet actual user needs. The experimentations in libraries, together with patrons, and peer libraries will help to better design, conduct, monitor and evaluate the experimentations. The experimentation outcome will help to make adoption decisions and leverage experiences for conducting further experimentations with AI technology landscape.

AI Experimentation Policies for Libraries: Ensuring Ethical Experimentation, M&E, and Structured Reporting in Business Support Services—Insights from Real Cases

This chapter explores how libraries can responsibly integrate artificial intelligence (AI) through structured experimentation policies, monitoring and evaluation (M&E), and ethical guidelines. It outlines the need for clear policies that promote innovation while ensuring compliance with data privacy regulations and ethical standards. The focus is on responsible experimentation in high-impact service areas, helping libraries balance opportunity with accountability. To support effective AI adoption, the chapter also introduces M&E mechanisms that guide libraries in tracking outcomes, capturing insights, and making data-informed decisions. These practices enable continuous improvement in library services and help shape future AI strategies. This chapter also provides a case study of a library that experimented with an AI text-to-video generator *(Controlled experimentation, as the business expert shared personal information, including his shared text, and the picture for digital avatar, for the video generation)*, along with the completed experimentation outcome template shared with library managers.

AI experimentation policy for Libraries: Balancing Innovation and Data Privacy
Gupta (2024e) presents a well-structured AI experimentation policy designed as part of the consulting project with library to help them experiment with artificial intelligence for possible integration of valuable ones into their business support services while ensuring ethical compliance and data privacy. The study underscores the necessity of categorizing AI experiments based on two primary factors: *the sensitivity of the data involved (Data sharing necessity)* and the *frequency with which the task requiring AI support occurs (Library task frequency)*. This categorization enables a strategic approach to experimentation, ensuring that innovations are pursued without compromising data security or ethical considerations.

V. Gupta, *Libraries as Hubs for Entrepreneurship*, Synthesis Lectures on Information Concepts, Retrieval, and Services, https://doi.org/10.1007/978-3-032-03569-1_7

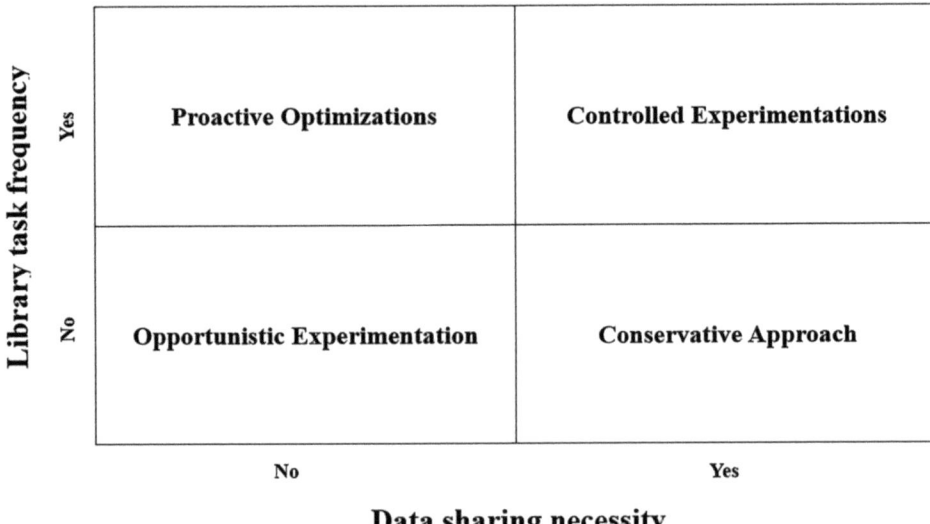

Fig. 7.1 AI Experimentation strategies framework matrix (Gupta, 2024e) (© 2024 Varun Gupta, reprinted by permission of Taylor & Francis Ltd., http://www.tandfonline.com)

It also provides the AI experimentation strategies framework, based on a two-dimensional model of library task frequency and data-sharing necessity, categorizes experimentation into four distinct approaches namely *Proactive Optimization, Controlled Experimentation, Opportunistic Experimentation, and Conservative Approach (Fig. 7.1).*

These experimentation strategies are briefly discussed below:

- **Proactive Optimization** is the most open and dynamic experimentation category. It applies to library tasks that occur frequently and do not involve sensitive data. Since these tasks are part of routine operations—such as improving teaching guides or designing entrepreneurship support materials—they provide librarians with an excellent opportunity to freely explore how AI tools, like ChatGPT or AI writing assistants, can enhance the quality and accessibility of their services. This type of experimentation can be done independently, with no approval required, and focuses on continuous improvement based on librarian initiative.
- **Controlled Experimentation** applies when the task is frequent but involves handling or sharing sensitive data, such as patron records or tailored business reports. In these cases, data protection becomes a priority. Librarians must follow rigorous protocols, including anonymizing data, using secure environments (such as AI sandboxes), and obtaining formal approvals before proceeding. The goal is to test AI applications while complying with ethical and legal requirements related to data privacy and consent.

- **Opportunistic Experimentation** refers to scenarios where tasks are performed infrequently and do not require the handling of sensitive data. These include ad hoc or seasonal projects, such as generating creative promotional content for one-time entrepreneurship workshops. Such experimentation is typically curiosity-driven and flexible, carried out when an opportunity presents itself or when the librarian sees an experimental value.
- **Conservative Approach** is for low-frequency tasks that involve sensitive data. These situations carry the highest risk and lowest recurrence. Unless there is a very strong business or ethical rationale, AI experimentation in these areas should be avoided. When absolutely necessary, experimentation should be approached with the highest level of scrutiny, layered approvals, and safeguards.

This classification not only provides practical guidance for library AI experimentation but also promotes innovation while ensuring ethical safeguards are respected. In case of controlled experimentations, it is mandatory to follow AI experimentation policy (Table 7.1) supported Controlled AI experimentation protocol (Table 7.2) as per, and Controlled AI experimentation approval and reporting form (Table 7.3) for necessary approvals as well as reporting. The AI experimentation policy provides necessary guidelines and principles for conducting AI technology-related experiments in the libraries with more controls on controlled experimentations, and more autonomy for those that don't involve sensitive data. Controlled Experimentation Protocol, which sets forth a structured approach for AI-related experiments. This protocol requires librarians to assess data sensitivity, review privacy policies, obtain management approvals for sensitive data experiments, and document experimentation results. By addressing these aspects, the study provides a framework that ensures AI experimentation remains responsible, well-documented, and aligned with the broader mission of libraries in supporting entrepreneurship and digital transformation. Additionally, in either experimentation, it is mandatory to systematically document the outcomes of AI experimentations in a template called structured Experimentation Outcome Sharing Template (Table 7.4), which then could be shared with peers for knowledge sharing fostering further experimentations and fostering M&E of the experimentation impacts.

The AI experimentation policy, Controlled AI experimentation protocol, and Controlled AI experimentation approval and reporting form are tabulated in Tables 7.1, 7.2, and 7.3.

Another major insight from this study is the emphasis on capacity-building for librarians. Many librarians are unfamiliar with the nuances of AI ethics, risk assessment, and privacy regulations, which can hinder the successful deployment of AI in libraries. The study recommends targeted training programs covering data privacy fundamentals, ethical AI usage, and risk assessment methodologies for evaluating AI tools before deployment.

Table 7.1 AI experimentation policy (Gupta, 2024e) (© 2024 Varun Gupta, reprinted by permission of Taylor & Francis Ltd., http://www.tandfonline.com)

Purpose: This policy outlines the guidelines and principles for experimenting with AI technologies in the library, ensuring that such experiments are conducted responsibly, ethically, and in alignment with the organization's policies and existing regulations

Scope: This policy applies to all AI-related experimentation within the library, including those that require sharing sensitive as well as non-sensitive AI technology. This policy does not apply for the implementation of the AI technology post successful experimentations. It covers all data types, with particular focus on sensitive data, and applies to all staff involved in AI-related projects

Guiding Principles
- **Ethical AI Use**: All AI experiments must adhere to ethical standards, ensuring fairness, transparency, and accountability
- **Data Protection**: Safeguarding patron and organizational data is paramount. Experiments involving sensitive data require heightened security measures
- **Compliance**: All AI activities must comply with relevant legal requirements, organizational policies, and data protection regulations

AI Experimentation Strategies
This policy is guided by a 2 × 2 matrix based on two variables: Library Task Frequency and Data Sharing Necessity (sensitive data). The following strategies correspond to different combinations of these variables:
- **Proactive Optimization**
  - **Application**: Frequent library tasks with no data-sharing necessity
  - **Strategy**: Encourage frequent experimentation to library frequent tasks, for instance, improving the teaching guides (e.g., systematic literature review guides). Librarian is free to conduct any experimentation and must share the details of experimentations and its outcome on library knowledge sharing platform
- **Controlled Experimentation**
  - **Application**: Frequent library tasks with high data-sharing necessity
  - **Strategy**: Implement AI cautiously, ensuring all experimental data is properly anonymized or synthetic data is used, in-house AI sandboxed are used (if available), and access to other data is restricted. Requires prior approval, close monitoring, and sharing details of conducted experimentations. Experimentation should be conducted as per approval conditions
- **Opportunistic Experimentation**
  - **Application**: Infrequent tasks with low data-sharing necessity
  - **Strategy**: Allow flexible experimentation to explore new AI applications that could enhance less frequent tasks, like generating customized content for specific queries. Librarians have full flexibility to decide which experiments to conduct and when; but it is recommended only when there is a business case to undertake these, owing to limited resources library processes
- **Conservative Approach**
  - **Application**: Infrequent tasks with high data-sharing necessity
  - **Strategy**: Limit or avoid experimentation unless there is a strong business case. If experimentation is necessary, apply the highest level of scrutiny and obtain explicit approvals as done for controlled experimentations

Data Handling and Privacy
- **Data Classification**: Librarians must classify data according to sensitivity levels before any AI experimentation. The existing library classifications can be used. In case particular data is not classified, use the library classification policy
- **Data Processing and Retention**: AI tools must process data in line with the library's data retention policies. In no case the librarians will use the full dataset available with the libraries. The data handling procedures need to be mentioned for getting approvals for the experimentations involving sensitive data. The experimentation samples should be completely anonymized, or synthetic data could be used. The technology policies, for instance privacy policy and terms of use, should be reviewed to understand data handling practices

Risk Management
- **Risk Assessment**: All AI experiments *(those requiring sensitive data)* must undergo a risk assessment to identify potential privacy, security, ethical risks, data Retention Issues, third party sharing risks. The risk assessment will be done by the librarian willing to undertake AI experiments

Experimentations Monitoring and Evaluation
- All the successful and failed experiments must be documented, including objectives, key success indicators, details of experimentation *(prompts used, data shared with AI tool, outcomes, data handling practices)*, recommendations, and lessons learned. The details should be shared with the management and uploaded on library knowledge sharing platform. The monitoring and evaluation committee will continuously monitor the experimentations and may conduct evaluations *(formative and summative)* to see if the experimentations were able to meet library improvisation objectives. A post-experimentation review should be conducted to assess effectiveness and identify lessons learned

Training, Awareness, and Institutional support
- **Staff Training**: Librarians and staff involved in AI experimentation must be trained on the AI policy, data protection practices, ethical AI use, and design and conducting the experimentations
- **Knowledge dissemination skills and training**: Librarians will receive training on effectively disseminating experimentation details, outcomes, and lessons learned to their peers. This training will equip librarians with the skills needed to share insights and foster a culture of continuous experimentation. By promoting knowledge sharing, the training also supports both formative and summative evaluations, encouraging other librarians to engage in and build upon these experiments
- **Continuous Learning**: Encourage ongoing education about advancements in AI technologies, evolving best practices in data protection and ethics, and learning from the peer's experimentations
- **Institutional support**: Librarians will receive support from both technical and legal teams. The technical team will assist with AI sandbox environments (if available), provide guidance on the AI technology under consideration, and manage the knowledge-sharing platform. The legal team will help librarians analyse technology contracts and navigate relevant data regulations

Policy Review
- This AI Experimentation Policy will be reviewed annually or as needed to accommodate new AI technologies, legal requirements, and organizational changes. Revisions will be made to ensure the policy remains relevant and effective

Table 7.2 Controlled AI experimentation protocol (Gupta, 2024e) (© 2024 Varun Gupta, reprinted by permission of Taylor & Francis Ltd., http://www.tandfonline.com)

After identifying that sensitive data needs to be shared with the AI technology (based on the organization's data classification policy) for a highly frequent library task, the librarian should follow these steps to seek management approval and conduct experimentation in strict accordance with approval conditions

---

1. **Review Privacy and Contractual Documents**: Examine the technology's privacy policy and contractual documents to understand data processing, AI model training, data ownership, and retention practices. This will help the librarian to consider only those technologies for experimentation that has lowest risks associated with retaining shared data, for using it for training its AI models, and sharing with third parties
2. **Manage Experimentation Data**: If technology does not use sensitive data for training and does not retain information, decide on using synthetic or anonymized data, and assess the need for patron consent. The decision should only pertain to experimentation and not adoption of the technology. For instance, librarian would like to experiment with the AI technologies for automating the customer requests for updated market research reports, for which sensitive data will be required. In this case, librarian can use synthetic data that mirrors the characteristics of actual data or anonymized data (that does not represent the real patron). During real implementation, patron consent will be necessary. Although current experimentation may be preliminary, it provides valuable insights and experience that can support future experimentation and potential adoption of AI technologies
3. **Seek Management Approval**: Use the Controlled AI Experimentation approval form (Table 7.3) and submit it to management for approval, including details on data characterises, data protection measures, consent requirements, experimentation objectives, indicators, and risk assessment
4. **Conduct Experimentation**: Execute the experiment under the approved conditions, adhering to all data handling and privacy protocols. Use the controlled environment, for instance AI sandbox if provided by the IT team
5. **Report Results**: Document and report the results of the experimentation to management, highlighting how sensitive data was managed, outcome of the experimentations, and any implications for future adoption. Use the Section 9 to 11 of Table 7.3 to report the findings
6. **Share the result**: Report on library knowledge platforms to provide insights and valuable information to other librarians for their reference and future experimentation

---

Structured Reporting of AI experimentations policy for fostering Knowledge sharing, future experimentations and Monitoring and Evaluations

Gupta (2024f) research work builds on the previous work by Gupta (2024e) by introducing a structured reporting mechanism that helps libraries document AI experimentation outcomes effectively. This study focuses on the importance of standardized reporting templates to facilitate peer learning, managerial assessments, and long-term monitoring and evaluation of AI initiatives. A core output of this study is the Experimentation Outcome Sharing Template (Table 7.4), which provides a consistent format for reporting AI trials. The template includes essential details such as experimentation objectives, success indicators, qualitative and quantitative outcomes, and reflections on AI limitations such as biases, hallucinations, ethical concerns, and black-box issues.

Table 7.3 Controlled AI experimentation approval and reporting form (Gupta 2024e) (© 2024 Varun Gupta, reprinted by permission of Taylor & Francis Ltd., http://www.tandfonline.com)

This form is to be filled and submitted to the library management through the manager for necessary approvals for conducting the controlled experimentation with sensitive data. Please fill Sections 1 to 7 for the approval, and 9 to 11 for reporting the experimentation results

1. **Basic Information**
   - Librarian Name:
   - Department:
   - Date:
2. **Technology Details**
   - AI Technology Name:
   - Provider:
   - Version:
   - Brief Description (*What does the AI tool do, and how will it be used?*)
3. **Data Classification**
   - Type of Sensitive Data Involved: (e.g., personal information, proprietary data)
   - Data Classification Status: (as per organisation classification)
   - Details of the data (*what data will be used*)
4. **Privacy and Contractual Review**
   - Privacy Policy Review*: (Yes/No)*
   - Contractual Documents Reviewed: *(Yes/No)*
   - Key Findings: (*e.g., data retention practices, data usage for AI model training, ownership of inputs and outputs, data shared with third parties*)
5. **Experimentation Data Management**
   - Type of Data to be used for Experimentation: (*e.g., synthetic data, anonymized data*)
   - Is Patron Consent Required for experimentation? *(Yes/No)*
   - Details on Data Management: (*e.g., methods used for anonymization, data handling procedures*)
6. **Experimentation Plan**
   - Objectives of Experimentation:
   - Key Indicators for Success:
7. **Risk and Compliance Summary**
Key Risks Identified (*if any*) and probability of occurrence (1 to 5; 5 means highest):
   - Data Breach: Risk of unauthorized access to sensitive data
   - Privacy Violations: Potential misuse of personal information if not properly anonymized
   - Data Retention Issues: Data stored longer than necessary, increasing vulnerability
   - Inaccurate AI Outputs: Risk of the AI generating misleading or incorrect information based on sensitive data
   - Others (*if any*)
(*The library will focus on technologies that does not retain the shared data, does not use it for training its AI models, and does not allow sharing with third parties. However, depending on the data handling procedures as reported by the librarians, exceptions can be made*)
8. **Management Approval**
   - Approval Status: (Approved/Denied)
   - Conditions for Approval:
   - Date of approval:
9. **Implementation Details**
   - Controlled Environment Used: (e.g., AI sandbox)
   - Experiment Start Date:
   - Experiment End Date:
   - Details of experimentation (*prompts used, data shared with AI tool, outcomes, recommendations, and lessons learned, others*)
10. **Reporting**
   - Report Submission Date:
   - Results Summary (*with interaction screenshots*):
   - Implications for Future Adoption:
11. **Other Relevant Information**

Note Submitting this form for reporting (Sections 9–11) still requires the librarian to complete the Structured Experimentation Outcome Sharing Template (Table 7.4). This template serves as the primary tool for systematically documenting experimentation activities and supports effective monitoring and evaluation (M&E) of the Digital Transformation program's experimentation interventions. It captures detailed information about the experimentation process in line with established M&E standards and practices. Additionally, it mentions how you managed to undertake the experimentation as per experimentation proposal shared for management approval (Sections 1–7)

Table 7.4 AI experimentation reporting template for Text-to-Video experimentation (adapted from (Gupta, 2024f) (© 2024 Varun Gupta, reprinted by permission of Taylor & Francis Ltd., http://www.tandfonline.com)

This document helps librarians to systematically document and share their AI experimentations with peers and management. This document can be used to share outcome of any type of experimentation

1. **Basic Information**
   - **Librarian Name**: [Redacted]
   - **Department**: [Redacted]
   - **Date**: [Redacted]
2. **Technology Details**
   - **AI Technology Name**: [Redacted]
   - **Provider**: [Redacted]
   - **Version**: [Redacted]
   - **Brief Description** (*Briefly describe the AI technology, its purpose, key features, and functionalities.*)

   The AI technology enables the conversion of user-specified text into realistic videos. Users can either upload their own photo to generate a personalized avatar or opt for a generic, non-human representation. The system supports multilingual input and can incorporate user-provided voice samples to produce natural-sounding speech. As a result, it creates lifelike videos tailored to various audiences—without the need for cameras, microphones, or production crews
3. **Controlled Experimentation Protocol**
   - **Protocol Number:** (*as provided by management at the time of approval*) CE-LIB-AI-03

   Note: The experimentation was conducted in-house in 2023, prior to the introduction of the formal controlled experimentation protocol established in 2024. The librarian ensured ethical standards by obtaining informed consent from participants and sharing only non-sensitive scripts, as provided by the entrepreneurs and himself (refer to previous discussion). No official protocol number was issued, as the formal system was not yet in place; the number referenced pertains to an internal record maintained by the library for documentation and outcome tracking

   This protocol number will help your peers and management to access the AI approved Experimentation approval application at library sharing platform
4. **Experimentation Objectives and Success Indicators**
   - **Objectives of Experimentation**

   Ensure to link the experimentation objectives with the broader goals of the library's digital transformation program, to foster effectiveness and impact of these interventions, and for facilitating further program evaluations

   The experimentations have the following objective:
     – To assess the effectiveness of AI-generated text-to-video content in improving user engagement on library social media platforms and event webpages within a four-week period
   - **Key Indicators for Success**
     – **Qualitative Indicators:** *Describe any qualitative measures used to gauge the success of the experiments*
       Expressions of interest by other librarians to explore similar AI tools
       Informal mentions and feedback from patrons, faculty, and staff about the videos
     – **Quantitative Indicators:** *List any quantitative metrics or data points used to evaluate the success*
       Number of Likes, Shares, and Comments on social media posts
       Average Time Spent on the event webpage
5. **Outcomes**
   - **Qualitative Outcomes:** *Summarize any qualitative findings from the experiment*
     – Positive informal feedback from students, entrepreneurs, and peer librarians about the video content
     – Several patrons shared the videos links externally via WhatsApp and Instagram
     – Peer librarians expressed interest in integrating similar tools in academic promotions
   - **Quantitative Outcomes:** *Present quantitative data and metrics gathered during the experiment*
     – *Average likes per post increased by 63%*
     – *Shares per post grew by 78%*
     – *Comments per post rose by 75%*
     – *Average time spent on the event webpage more than doubled (from 42 s to 1 min 36 s)*
   - **Value Generated for the library:** *Describe the value or benefits derived from the experiment (if implemented) for the specific use case for the library task*
     Demonstrated the viability of AI-generated videos in improving patron engagement and promotional outreach. Sparked peers' curiosity in adopting AI-driven services. Positioned the library as an innovator in AI experimentation for patron communication. Finally, it will generate curiosities to experiment with other AI technologies which are cost effective, easy to use, and generates value to the library without the need for procuring new infrastructure
6. **Justifications**
   - *Provide reasons why the experimentation should be considered valuable, even if it did not produce the expected outcomes*
   The experimentation was valuable as with minimal efforts, it created informative videos about the entrepreneurship events that innovated the ways library communicate about these events with patrons. It sparked new applications areas of this technology in library and curiosities to experiment with similar technologies too
   - *To build trust about your findings, explain how you managed the known AI limitations, for instance,*
   - **Biases** (*systematic errors in AI models that reflect prejudices in training data, leading to unfair or skewed outcomes*)
   To avoid potential representation biases, only neutral, professional, and culturally inclusive avatars and voice options were selected. No stereotyped, gendered, or culturally loaded visuals or voices were used. All scripts were written in neutral, inclusive language to ensure fair and unbiased communication
   - **Instabilities** (*variations in AI output due to minor changes in input data, affecting the consistency and reliability of decisions/outcomes*)
   No noticeable instabilities were observed during the experiment. The text-to-video AI system produced consistent outputs for identical or similar text inputs, with stable avatar behaviour, voice modulation, and synchronization across repeated renders. As a precaution, videos were previewed to confirm output consistency before public release
   - **Hallucinations** (*instances where AI generates plausible but incorrect or nonsensical information*)
   No auto-generated visual or verbal content was allowed. All video scripts were manually written and uploaded into the system by the librarian. Text-to-video outputs were manually reviewed to ensure the visuals and voiceover accurately reflected the script. No AI-generated content was used
   - **Black-box issue** (*lack of transparency in AI systems, making it difficult to understand or explain how decisions are made*)
   While the AI system's internal processes for pairing avatars, voices, and animations are not transparent, all final video outputs were manually reviewed to validate synchronization between video, lip movements, and spoken content
   - **Ethical issues** (*concerns related to the fairness, privacy*)
   Informed consent was obtained from all individuals for the use of their photos as digital avatars and for public release of the AI-generated videos. They also formally declared that the provided text scripts could be used for public distribution within these videos
   - **Unknowns** (*unidentified issues or blind spots in AI models that could lead to unexpected outcomes*)
   Nothing was observed. It will be interesting to see how the technology will work for other natural languages
7. **Lesson learned**
   - **Key Insights:** *Summarize the critical insights gained from the experiment, focusing on what worked, what didn't, and why*
     – AI-generated videos substantially increased engagement, confirming that curiosity-led trials can yield valuable service innovations
     – The CBE framework enabled a low-risk, highly insightful experiment
     – Early skepticism from staff was replaced with enthusiasm following tangible results
   - **Recommendations:** *Offer suggestions that could be useful for future experiments in libraries, including any changes or improvements that could enhance outcomes*
     – Integrate AI-generated video promotions into routine library communications, especially for events, announcements, and service updates
     – Extend experimentation to other AI tools such as text-to-speech, video summarization, and AI captioning for inclusive content delivery
     – Foster a culture of experimentation through shared blogs, reference guides, and structured CBE outcome templates
8. **Conclusion**
   - *Recap the experiment's overall impact on the library's operations and its alignment with broader strategic goals. Also, outline any planned follow-up actions or further experiments that will build on the current findings*
   This experimentation demonstrated the practical value of integrating AI-generated videos in promoting library services, significantly enhancing patron engagement while fostering a culture of AI exploration. This experimentation will foster further experimentations of using this and similar technologies for various library marketing activities without the need for sophisticated infrastructure and involvement of marketing departments. The outcomes directly support the library's digital transformation objective of enhancing digital communication and outreach. Moving forward, the library plans to formalize AI-generated video use for service promotions, trial additional AI tools, and establish routine documentation and sharing of AI experimentation outcomes for M&E
   - *Include any relevant documents, for instance, screenshots of the prompt screen. data sets, for instance insights brought from AI tool and other technologies, or supplementary materials*
   Relevant screenshots, prompt records, and analytics reports have been archived with this documentation [Redacted]

Table 7.4 presents the AI experimentation reporting template based on the documentation of a text-to-video experimentation conducted in one of the libraries (see Chap. 6), where a librarian—motivated by curiosity—began using text-to-video generators to enhance social media engagement for entrepreneurship support events. At the time of the experimentation, a structured reporting template was not available except the free form template for formulation of the business case. However, the template has been retrospectively populated for this case, as detailed information was accessible due to the author's involvement as a consultant. The purpose of this example is to illustrate how such reporting templates can be completed and presented to library managers. As discussed in Chap. 6, the experimentation involved some sensitive data especially avatars of the people featured in the video, and introductory contents of the entrepreneurship events to attract participants. The experimentation was conducted in controlled manner, with the requirement taking explicit informed consent from those featuring in the video. These people signed a declaration affirming that they had the right to make the statements public or had obtained necessary permissions from third parties, as well as consent to use their digital avatars in the videos. As per the AI experimentation policy, this experimentation falls under the category of controlled experimentation. This is because the task of the promotion of library events is a recurring responsibility and hence was a high-frequency activity. Second, the content created involved sensitive data, like contents, and avatars. Table 7.4 shows the AI experimentation reporting template for Text-to-Video experimentation, grounded on the experimentation execution and outcome details available in the documentations.

AI experimentation reporting template support for M&E

The structured reporting form plays a pivotal role in embedding Monitoring and Evaluation (M&E) processes within AI experimentations in libraries by ensuring that each experimental activity is systematically aligned with the overarching Theory of Change (ToC) of the library's digital transformation (DT) program. It does so by requiring librarians to clearly define individual experimentation objectives, anticipated outputs, and intended outcomes—core ToC elements—and explicitly link them to the DT program's broader objectives, outputs, and outcomes. This alignment not only helps in clarifying the intervention logic behind each AI trial but also makes it easier to assess how individual experiments contribute to the program's short, medium, and long-term goals.

The structured reporting form serves as a foundational M&E tool that supports both formative and summative evaluations within AI experimentations aligned to library digital transformation programs. In formative evaluations, the reports act as real-time monitoring instruments, capturing indicators of change such as progress towards intended outputs and early signs of desired outcomes, depending on the specific objectives of each experiment. These insights allow for continuous adjustments, helping librarians and managers refine interventions as they progress. For summative evaluations, the outcome reporting forms offer rich, structured evidence for assessing the overall effectiveness, relevance, and contribution of AI experiments to the DT program's broader outcomes. Depending on the summative evaluation's focus, these reports can help identify potential librarians to involve as key informants or participants in endline evaluations. Additionally, for assessing the downstream outcomes—particularly the impact on patrons—it would require librarians to conduct follow-up surveys, focus groups, or case studies with patrons who have engaged with services or programs built upon successfully tested AI technologies. This integrated reporting and evaluation process ensures not just technological adoption, but meaningful, evidence-based improvements in library services and user experiences.

Moreover, by structuring experimentation outcomes around qualitative and quantitative success indicators, value generation, and lessons learned, the form strengthens the M&E system's capacity to evaluate both effectiveness and relevance of AI interventions within the DT program. It essentially turns experimentation into a managed intervention cycle, where each AI pilot can be evaluated against both its own ToC and the program's collective ToC, ensuring coherence, alignment, and cumulative impact measurement over time.

Key Insights and Concluding Reflections

A key insight from the research by Gupta (2024f) is the importance of cross-institutional knowledge-sharing. The study highlights that structured reports should not only be used internally but also shared on platforms like LibGuides and Open Educational Resources repositories. This approach fosters collaboration among libraries, reduces redundancy in experimentation, and accelerates the adoption of best practices. The study also stresses the necessity of aligning AI experimentation with library-wide digital transformation strategies. Rather than conducting isolated AI trials, librarians should ensure that each experiment supports broader institutional goals, such as enhancing business research support services, improving entrepreneurship programs, and developing AI-driven digital tools.

When analyzed together, the findings from Gupta (2024e, 2024f) present a comprehensive framework for AI experimentation in library business support services. The first article provides a policy-driven approach, while the second article builds upon it with a structured reporting system to institutionalize experimentation outcomes. One major area of convergence is the role of Monitoring and Evaluation. The first study positions M&E as a governance tool to ensure compliance and assess AI's experimentation outputs (as expected by the librarian at the time of designing the experimentation aligned with overall Digital transformation program of the library for enhancing their business support services) as well as its long-term impact, whereas the second study presents structured reporting as the mechanism that enables effective M&E practices. Together, these perspectives create a robust system where AI experimentation is not only policy-driven but also transparently monitored and continuously improved upon.

Another key area of alignment is the emphasis on librarian training. Both studies recognize that librarians need specialized skills in AI ethics, privacy regulations, and risk management. Without adequate training, even the most structured policies and reporting mechanisms could fall short of their intended impact.

From a practical perspective, the combined findings highlight several crucial aspects that should be integrated into AI experimentation policies for libraries. Ethical and regulatory compliance must be prioritized to ensure that AI experimentation aligns with institutional policies and data protection laws. AI experimentation should be embedded within a broader M&E framework to facilitate continuous assessment, ensuring that structured documentation and reporting inform future AI adoption strategies. A uniform Experimentation Outcome Sharing Template ensures consistency in reporting AI trials, and making reports accessible through institutional knowledge-sharing platforms can foster cross-library collaboration. Librarians should be trained in AI ethics, risk assessment, and privacy policies, with training also covering practical AI experimentation methods that enable librarians to make informed decisions about AI adoption. AI trials should not be conducted in isolation but should support broader library transformation objectives, ensuring they contribute to institutional strategic goals such as business research support and digital entrepreneurship programs.

Enhancing Library Business Support Through AI Tools: Practical Applications of ASReview, Connected Papers, and Citation Gecko in Real Cases

8

This chapter explores the use of AI-driven tools in enhancing library services for entrepreneurs. Specifically, it focuses on three tools—ASReview, Connected Papers, and Citation Gecko—that support systematic literature reviews, discovery of related research, and citation analysis. These tools help reduce the time and effort required to identify relevant academic resources, enabling entrepreneurs to make more informed business decisions.

Each section provides a brief discussion of the tools, highlights the benefits for both librarians and entrepreneurs, and shares lessons learned by libraries during their implementation. The lessons are drawn from consulting projects with libraries in improving their business support services by adopting these technologies. By integrating these AI tools into existing services, libraries can offer targeted research support, enable entrepreneurs to independently conduct literature-driven research, and do so while preserving user privacy and requiring minimal technical training. Through librarian guidance and co-creation with the entrepreneurs, these tools can be effectively adopted to enhance access to knowledge, improve research outcomes, and strengthen the role of libraries in supporting entrepreneurship. This chapter also provides a practical reference guide for using ASReview, Connected Papers, and Citation Gecko in library settings. These tools support entrepreneurs in discovering and applying research insights relevant to their business needs.

AI-driven systematic review tool (ASReview)

Gupta (2024g) explores the application of ASReview, an AI-driven systematic review tool, in supporting entrepreneurs through library services. It highlights how reference librarians play a crucial role in assisting entrepreneurs by guiding them toward relevant business

V. Gupta, *Libraries as Hubs for Entrepreneurship*, Synthesis Lectures on Information Concepts, Retrieval, and Services, https://doi.org/10.1007/978-3-032-03569-1_8

literature, offering technology recommendations, and conducting systematic reviews. The article showcases ASReview as an AI-powered tool that enables more efficient and targeted literature discovery, reducing the time and effort required for manual searches across bibliographic databases. The study reveals that ASReview employs active learning techniques, allowing users to label relevant and irrelevant articles, which helps the AI refine its ranking of unseen articles. This iterative process enhances the quality of literature recommendations provided to entrepreneurs. By integrating ASReview into library services, librarians can better assist entrepreneurs in identifying critical research materials, thus streamlining their decision-making processes.

A consulting project cited in the article demonstrated ASReview's effectiveness in delivering curated literature references about value proposition innovations to entrepreneurs. Additionally, a workshop using ASReview engaged entrepreneurs in hands-on sessions, enabling them to explore AI's potential for addressing business challenges. The findings suggest that ASReview can be seamlessly incorporated into library services due to its user-friendly interface, no privacy and data sharing issues (data is stored locally on the user computer), and minimal training requirements for librarians and patrons. This will help libraries to boost their reference services to the entrepreneurs, involve external subject matter experts for topic outside expertise of the business librarians, and help entrepreneur develop skills to use this technology on their won to solve their business information needs.

AI technologies like ASReview foster knowledge discovery, foster co-creation with librarians with domain expertise for correct labelling of articles, enhancing access to the library resources, for instance bibliographic database subscriptions. Figure 8.1 illustrates the training process of the model, while Figs. 8.2 and 8.3 depict the labelling of records as relevant or irrelevant following the initial training of the AI model.

A crucial insight from the study is that AI-driven tools like ASReview align with existing AI experimentation policies in libraries, as they do not require sharing sensitive data externally. This means librarians can integrate ASReview into their services without additional privacy concerns and could experiment with this easily together with entrepreneurs as well as external business support actors.

Connected Papers Tool

Gupta and Gupta (2023d) focuses on the use of Connected Papers, an AI-powered tool designed to help entrepreneurs and researchers navigate scholarly literature efficiently. This tool visually maps relationships between academic papers, enabling users to quickly identify relevant research clusters. This tool creates the graph of the connected papers based on Co-citation and Bibliographic Coupling and hence could provide meaningful insights about papers relevant to the entrepreneur information needs. The study emphasizes that Connected Papers accelerates information discovery by reducing the time spent on literature reviews while maintaining high research quality.

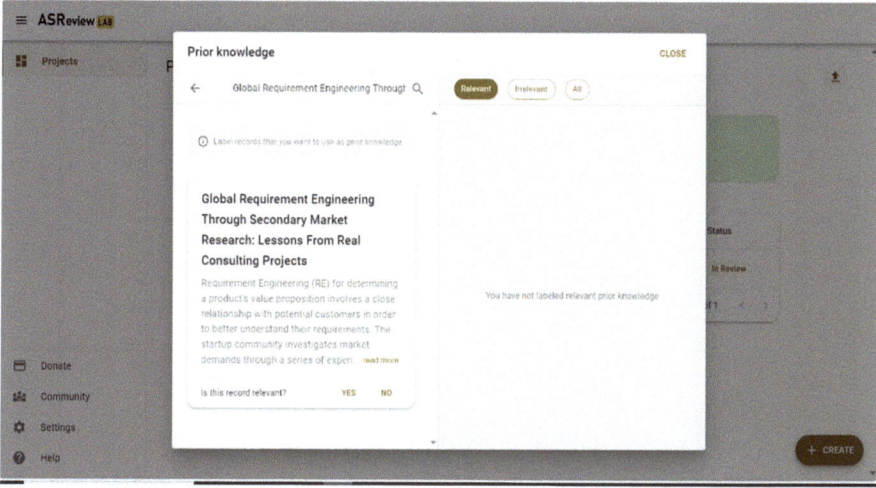

Fig. 8.1 Initial training of the model incorporating prior knowledge (Gupta 2024g) (© 2024 Varun Gupta, reprinted by permission of Taylor & Francis Ltd., http://www.tandfonline.com)

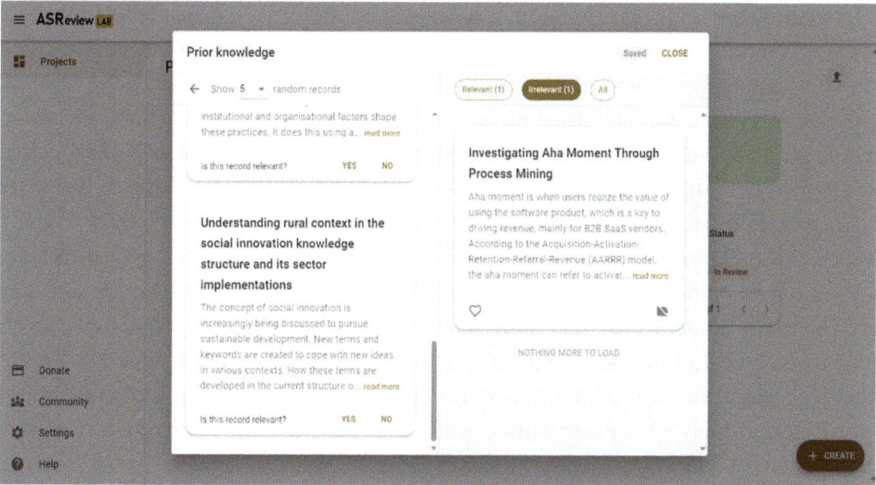

Fig. 8.2 Labeling of records as irrelevant after the model's initial training (Gupta 2024g) (© 2024 Varun Gupta, reprinted by permission of Taylor & Francis Ltd., http://www.tandfonline.com)

The article highlights how libraries are evolving into key players in entrepreneurial support ecosystems. By integrating AI-driven technologies like Connected Papers, libraries can provide enhanced research services tailored to business owners. Entrepreneurs benefit

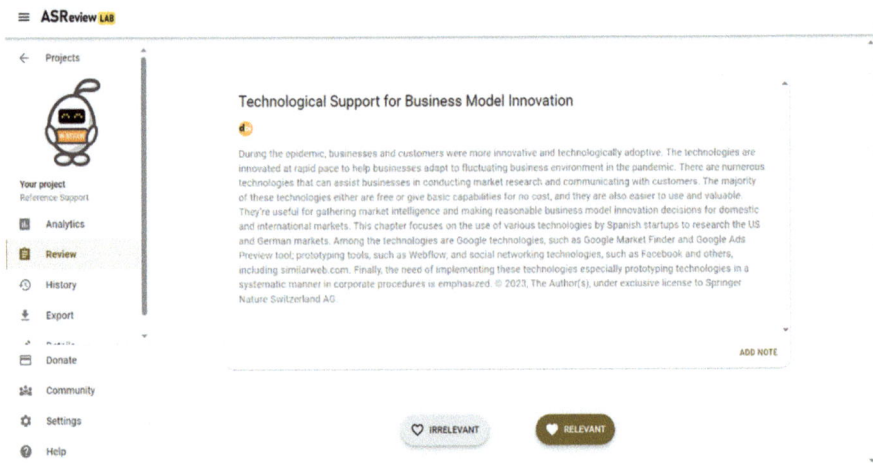

Fig. 8.3 Labeling of records as relevant following the model's initial training (Gupta 2024g) (© 2024 Varun Gupta, reprinted by permission of Taylor & Francis Ltd., http://www.tandfonline.com)

from this tool by accessing structured knowledge networks that help them refine their business strategies, navigate the research landscape pertaining to the business topic to meet business information need, and identify research-backed solutions to business challenges.

Another notable outcome of this study is the introduction of entrepreneurial stages in relation to systematic literature reviews. The research outlines various phases of an entrepreneur's journey, such as the development phase and operational phase, and discusses how systematic reviews can support entrepreneurs at different stages. For instance, early-stage entrepreneurs might require systematic literature reviews to validate their business ideas or to explore foundational research, while growth-stage entrepreneurs may use them to explore market expansion strategies or to identify emerging trends and innovations. The study underscores the importance of librarian training in AI tools to ensure effective implementation and maximize the value provided to entrepreneurs. Figure 8.4 presents the graph for one of the papers on entrepreneurship during the pandemic *(seed paper)*. Figure 8.5 displays prior works, while Fig. 8.6 illustrates derivative works.

A significant takeaway from the research is that Connected Papers could foster a culture of continuous learning and experimentation as the librarian support is crucial in getting expert advise about seed papers, technology usage guides, entrepreneurial skills, and interpretations of the results. The AI-enhanced research tools like Connected Papers serve as a bridge between academic knowledge and real-world business applications, making libraries indispensable resources for business innovation. This will enable business reference librarians to apply their business and research expertise for the successful adoption of this technology, while also enhancing their skills based on interactions with

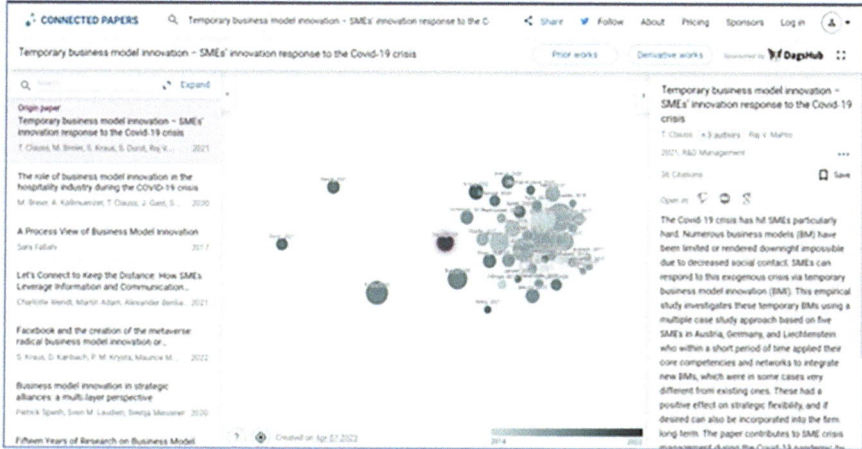

Fig. 8.4 Network Graph of Similar Articles about entrepreneurship during the pandemic using Connected Papers technology (Gupta and Gupta 2023d) (Copyright © 2023, Emerald Publishing Limited, reprinted by permission of Emerald Publishing Limited, https://www.emerald.com/)

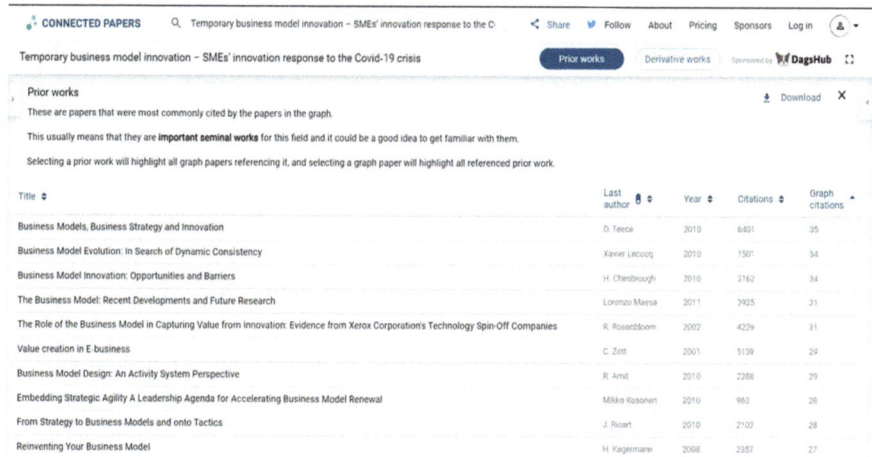

Fig. 8.5 Prior works List generated by Connected Papers technology (Gupta and Gupta 2023d) (Copyright © 2023, Emerald Publishing Limited, reprinted by permission of Emerald Publishing Limited, https://www.emerald.com/)

technology as well as the entrepreneurs, to support continuous ongoing engagement and broader applications of the tool for meeting diverse information needs of the businesses.

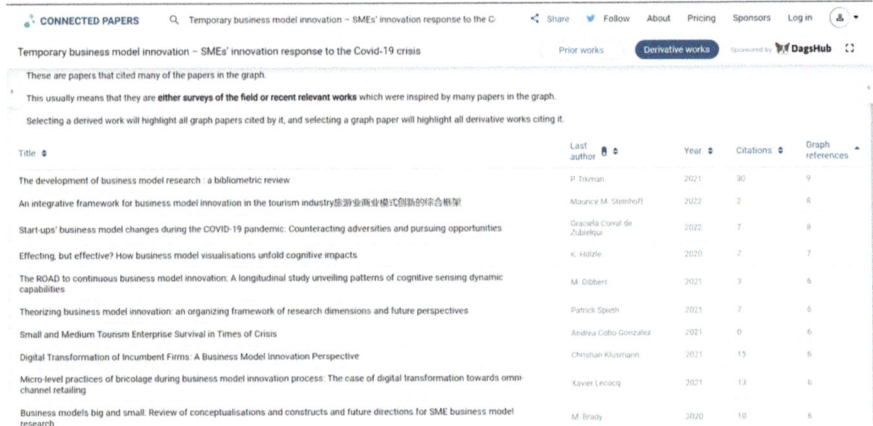

Fig. 8.6 Derivative Works List generated by Connected Papers technology (Gupta and Gupta 2023d) (Copyright © 2023, Emerald Publishing Limited, reprinted by permission of Emerald Publishing Limited, https://www.emerald.com/)

Citation Gecko Tool

Gupta (2023c) introduces Citation Gecko, an AI-based citation analysis tool that helps entrepreneurs and researchers discover relevant academic papers through citation networks. The study emphasizes that Citation Gecko enhances systematic literature reviews by allowing users to track citation relationships, identify influential research works, and generate comprehensive bibliographies. The findings highlight that Citation Gecko simplifies the research process by automating backward and forward citation tracking. Entrepreneurs can use this tool to identify seminal works in their field and stay updated with the latest advancements that will help them make business decisions. Figure 8.7 shows the citation network based on the citations of the seed paper (multiple seed papers are possible) and those cited by the seed paper.

The study also underscores the role of librarians in guiding entrepreneurs on effective research strategies, including how to use AI tools like Citation Gecko, analysis of the accuracy of the conducted research using this tool, recommending possible seed papers. This is possible owing to the business reference librarian's business and research skills. Citation Gecko could complement traditional research methodologies by reducing the cognitive load associated with manual literature reviews. This tool is particularly beneficial for entrepreneurs who need to quickly synthesize academic knowledge to support their business decisions. AI-powered citation analysis will make the research process much easier and quick, could improve knowledge accessibility, and strengthens the role of libraries as innovation hubs for business support.

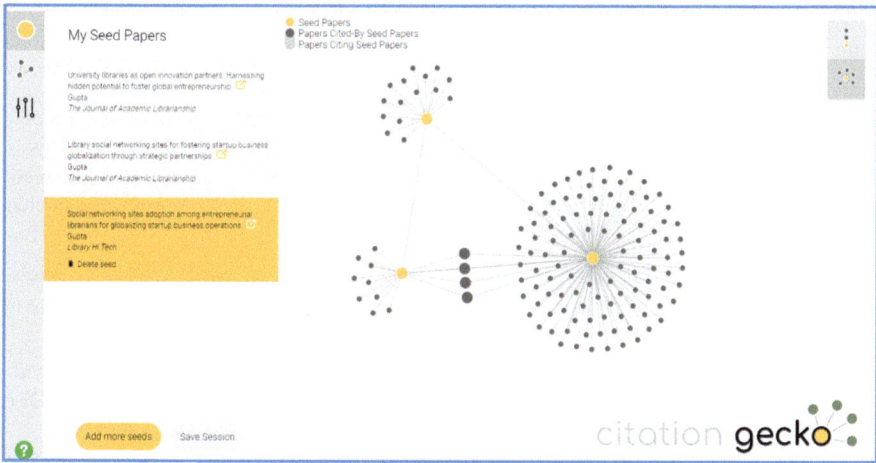

Fig. 8.7 Citation graph for papers cited by seed papers (Gupta 2023c) (Copyright © 2023, Emerald Publishing Limited, reprinted by permission of Emerald Publishing Limited, https://www.emerald.com/)

Comparative analysis of ASReview, Connected Papers, and Citation Gecko for Libraries Supporting Entrepreneurs

The technologies ASReview, Connected Papers, and Citation Gecko can be evaluated and compared across several key factors to help libraries effectively support entrepreneurs. These factors include **Primary Function** (the main purpose of the tool), **Best For** (the ideal use cases or user groups), **Input Needed** (the type and amount of data or documents required to start), **Offline Use** (whether the tool can function without internet connectivity), **Access to Full Articles** (availability of complete texts versus just metadata or abstracts), **Cost** (pricing models such as free, subscription, or pay-per-use), **Ethical and Privacy Issues** (concerns related to data security and user confidentiality), and the **Business Reference Librarian's Role** (how librarians can assist users in utilizing the tool effectively). By compressing the comparison along these dimensions, libraries can strategically select and integrate the most suitable technologies for facilitating entrepreneurs' research and innovation needs.

Table 8.1 presents a comparative overview of ASReview, Connected Papers, and Citation Gecko across key factors such as Primary Function, Best For, Input Needed, Offline Use, Access to Full Articles, Cost, Ethical/Privacy Issues, and the Business Reference Librarian's Role.

Library Reference Guide/Instruction material for ASReview, Connected Papers, and Citation Gecko for Entrepreneurs and other patrons

Entrepreneurs increasingly need to ground their ideas in research—whether it's exploring trends, validating business models, exploring innovative practices of other companies,

Table 8.1 Comparative analysis of ASReview, connected papers, and citation Gecko

Feature	AS review	Connected papers	Citation Gecko
Primary function	Prioritizes and ranks papers from large datasets using AI	Visual map of semantically similar research articles (via Co-citation and Bibliographic Coupling)	Graphical representation of research articles related to the seed paper through citations
Best for	Synthesizing evidence from bibliographic databases	Finding thematically related papers around a central topic	Mapping a topic's evolution, citing or cited works
Input needed	Large exported bibliographic datasets (e.g., from Scopus, web of science)	A known **seed paper** (title/DOI) or even the keyword	One or more seed papers (title/DOI or search through keyword)
Offline use	Yes. The software operates on the local server in an offline mode	No	No
Access to full articles	Not included. Users need to access non open access articles through their library membership or purchase them	Not included. Users need to access non open access articles through their library membership or purchase them	Not included. Users need to access non open access articles through their library membership or purchase them
Cost	Free and open source	Free (for 5 graphs per month)	Free
Ethical/privacy issues	No personal data used. Data is stored on local machine. Exporting of results (prioritised and ranked list) is possible	No login or personal data required. Results could be saved and seen later. It's possible to download as well	No login or personal data required. Results are not saved but could be exported
Business reference Librarian's role	Support for extracting dataset of articles post bibliographic database search, support in uploading datasets, advising on article labelling	Suggest seed articles, interpret graph, and recommend follow-up searches	Identify key seed papers and help to interpret graphs

or mapping prior knowledge. These three free tools—ASReview, Connected Papers, and Citation Gecko—can help you discover the right research efficiently. Librarians specialised in referencing, and research can play a vital role in facilitating access, guidance, and interpretation for meeting the information needs of the entrepreneurs from the research literature.

Use Cases for Entrepreneurs

- **ASReview** is perfect when you need comprehensive knowledge synbook (e.g., for investor pitches, white papers, or policy studies) from the research literature. You can quickly rank a large set of articles by relevance with minimal effort. From there, you can either conduct a systematic synbook or simply follow the top-ranked articles for deeper exploration.
- **Connected Papers** is great for identifying the semantically similar research articles based on article interest (called seed paper). This tool could provide you similar articles to your seed article even through they may not be directly citing each other. You can create the visual map with cluster of similar articles together, helping you to identify new ideas, for instance by revealing unexpected gaps or connections in the map. You can visualize the broader research landscape connected to your topic (via a seed paper) to better understand key developments—helping you apply research insights directly to your business practice.
- **Citation Gecko** helps you find the papers that cited the seed paper or those cited by the seed. The citation graph helps to navigate research landscape related to the seed paper and could give additional insights about growth or maturity of research line. his can be valuable for identifying relevant articles that address specific business information needs, or for gaining insight into the maturity or saturation of a business topic—such as pricing in underdeveloped markets—before making strategic decisions or taking action.

How to Use Each Tool

- **ASReview**

Note: Use when you have a large number of articles and want to prioritize the most relevant.

Steps:

- Export a bibliographic dataset (from Scopus, PubMed, etc.) as.csv or.ris. Datasets from other bibliographic databases are also supported.

- Visit https://asreview.nl and install the software on your local machine or use the library-hosted version. The installation procedure is available at https://asreview.nl/install/.
- Training stage: Upload your dataset and train your AI Model (Prior knowledge). This requires you to mark some dataset entries as relevant and irrelevant to train AI model.
- Screening Phase: Now start the screening process by labelling the articles as relevant or irrelevant. As this process continues, the tool re-ranks articles in real time, ensuring users always see the most up-to-date ordering.
- Export your ranked results for further actions.

Library Tip: Ask your librarian to install a local version for secure offline use, support for extracting dataset of articles post bibliographic database search, support in uploading datasets, advising on article labelling.

- **Connected Papers**

Note: Use when exploring a topic and want to discover similar research.

Steps:

- Go to https://connectedpapers.com. You can create your login account or continue without any login.
- Enter the title or DOI of a known article (your "seed paper"), or the keywords.
- Click "Build Graph".
- Explore the graph of related papers:
- Older foundational work on the left
- More recent derivatives on the right
- Click a node for abstract, link, and metadata.
- Download the list.

Library Tip: Seek librarian help in getting advice about the seed papers to get higher-quality maps.

- **Citation Gecko**

Note: Use when you want to explore what came before and after a paper (citations).

Steps:

- Go to https://citationgecko.azurewebsites.net.
- Paste one or more seed articles or search using search query.
- Click "Build Graph".

- Explore the graph of related papers:
- Backward citations (papers your seed cited).
- Forward citations (papers citing your seed).
- Export the list or use it for building bibliographies.

Library Tip: Seek librarian help in getting advice about the seed papers to get higher-quality results.

Access and Ethics

- All three tools are free to use, and safe from a privacy/legal standpoint, since they only work with publicly available paper metadata. Further, ASReview works on local machine and search data is stored locally. Other technologies don't require login (optional in connected papers technology).
- Full articles are not directly available through these tools. Libraries can assist with:
  - Licensed database access (*for those that are available in the library, or collaborating libraries*).
  - Interlibrary loan or document delivery.
  - Directing you to open access versions (if available) .

Role of the Librarian

Librarians bring domain expertise and research guidance that make these tools more effective for your entrepreneurship journey. The business reference librarian can support you in the following ways:

- Guide patrons in selecting seed papers based on topic and domain knowledge.
- Support dataset preparation and advising on article labelling. (for ASReview).
- Help interpret visual outputs and results.
- Provide access to full-text resources.
- Offer training, workshops, and consultations on integrating these tools into entrepreneurial projects.
- Advise about follow-up searches.
- Secure full-text access through the right library channels.
- Help you choose which tool to use based on your stage and needs.

Final Reflections on ASReview, Connected Papers, and Citation Gecko: Key Takeaways and Implementation Pathways for Library Service Innovation

The research studies by Gupta (2024g), Gupta and Gupta (2023d), and Gupta (2023c) collectively present a compelling case for the integration of AI technologies into library business support services. ASReview, Connected Papers, and Citation Gecko each offer unique functionalities that address different aspects of literature discovery and systematic reviews. While ASReview focuses on active learning to refine literature recommendations, Connected Papers provides visual mapping of research networks, and Citation Gecko enhances citation tracking for comprehensive bibliographic analysis. A significant convergence in all three studies is the emphasis on AI-driven research tools as enablers of entrepreneurial innovation. These tools collectively reduce the time and effort required for systematic literature reviews, allowing entrepreneurs to focus on applying research insights to their business challenges. Additionally, the studies highlight the evolving role of librarians as facilitators of AI-powered research, underscoring the need for continuous training in emerging technologies.

Another key takeaway is that AI tools enhance the accessibility of published scholarly knowledge, bridging the gap between scholarly research and practical business applications. By adopting AI-enhanced research services, libraries position themselves as critical partners in entrepreneurial ecosystems, fostering a culture of experimentation and continuous learning. The co-creation with the librarians is crucial to get skills to use these technologies, leverage the existing library resources, for instance bibliographic databases, and expert advise about the search process and the notable articles, to enhance the tool outcome value for meeting the business information needs.

Library managers need to focus on implementing AI-powered tools in research areas where they offer practical value. This involves adopting technologies like Citation Gecko, ASReview, and Connected Papers to help entrepreneurs efficiently navigate academic databases, extract meaningful information, and generate comprehensive literature maps. The challenge here is that despite an increasing volume of scholarly research on startups, entrepreneurs struggle to access, interpret, and apply academic insights due to fragmented publishing platforms, resource constraints, and differences in research and business priorities. Libraries do provide reference support where business librarians refer the information resources to the entrepreneurs, or research support to them. However, apart from the innovations required from the publishing venues, the open collaborations between libraries and other innovation ecosystem actors, for instance subject matter experts, industry practitioners could help startups to acquire practical insights from the bibliographic literature, especially from the practice articles. There are two main implications for library managers.

Library managers must actively promote technology experimentation within libraries, creating an environment that encourages knowledge sharing and collaborative learning. By fostering a culture of innovation, they can enable librarians and patrons to explore emerging technologies, assess their relevance, and refine their applications based on real-world feedback. Even on a smaller scale, implementing technologies with strong use cases can drive meaningful improvements in library services, enhancing research support, business assistance, and community engagement. Strategic experimentation ensures that libraries remain adaptable and forward-thinking, gradually integrating technologies that offer tangible benefits while minimizing risks associated with large-scale, untested deployments.

Library managers could felicitate research consultations by offering dedicated sessions where librarians act as knowledge mediators, helping entrepreneurs translate bibliographic literature into actionable business strategies. Library managers must expand their human resources by incorporating business reference librarians and those with expertise in entrepreneurship. These specialists will play a vital role in engaging with entrepreneurs through continuous interactions and tailored training programs, ensuring that library services align with the specific needs of business users. Rather than offering direct business solutions, their role is to provide well-researched, high-quality references that guide entrepreneurs toward relevant information sources. This approach empowers entrepreneurs to independently analyse and apply insights from business cases, scholarly articles, and other credible resources that align with their specific challenges, without prescribing specific implementation strategies. By fostering a knowledge-driven support system, libraries can enhance their role as facilitators of entrepreneurial success.

Implications for Library Managers

9

Library managers are at the forefront of digital transformation in business support services. Based on the findings of this research, the following implications address key areas where libraries can optimize their roles in fostering entrepreneurship by leveraging AI adoption, co-creation, and structured experimentation while addressing ethical considerations and including monitoring & evaluation (M&E) of their experimentations.

Strengthening Libraries' Role in Entrepreneurship Support

Library managers should begin offering business support services on a smaller scale, leveraging existing resources before expanding their capabilities. This aligns with the American Library Association's (American Library Association 2022) recommendation that libraries should at least start on a smaller scale for offering business support, leveraging their existing resources for this purpose. This means that even a smaller library could offer business support even at the smaller scale, and coordinate with medium and larger libraries to expand further. By doing so, libraries can assess demand, refine their approach, and gradually scale services based on community needs.

A key area for improvement is the development of stronger partnerships between academic and public libraries, a collaboration that remains underutilized. Given the differing priorities of these institutions—academic libraries focusing on research and education, while public libraries serve broader community needs—library managers must bridge this gap. Establishing structured academic-public library partnerships will provide aspiring entrepreneurs with seamless access to customized business support services. Academic library patrons, particularly students and researchers, can use their entrepreneurial skills gained in academic settings while tapping into public libraries for broader community-oriented business resources. Additionally, university-based business incubators and entrepreneurship centers—which focus on commercializing ideas—can complement public library services, ensuring that startups receive well-rounded support.

To facilitate this collaboration, library managers should consider appointing designated entrepreneurship librarians, similar to the approach at the University of Toronto (UofT), which however were refined for library entrepreneurial support coordination with the university. These librarians can coordinate business support efforts across academic and public libraries, ensuring that entrepreneurs receive specialized guidance tailored to their stage of business development. This structured coordination will improve knowledge transfer, expand resource accessibility, and create a unified ecosystem where both academic and public libraries contribute effectively to local entrepreneurial growth.

Library managers should establish resource-sharing agreements between academic and public libraries to optimize access to business-related materials. For instance, academic libraries subscriptions are not meant for commercial use while public libraries usually have licenses especially for the resources that are meant for the business support. A shared-access model would ensure that entrepreneurs, including the student entrepreneurs will benefit from the business support resources available in-house as well as those offered by the public libraries. Offering some joint training programs, starting with the common members of academic and public libraries will strengthen collaboration and knowledge sharing.

Library managers should collaborate with local government, business incubators, and economic development agencies to ensure that library business support aligns with broader entrepreneurial ecosystems. Public libraries can serve as access points for government grants and startup funding programs, while academic libraries can contribute university-backed entrepreneurship research and innovation resources, for instance in form of joint funded projects or regional development funded projects. This aligns with the third mission of the universities, which focuses on contributing to the social, cultural, and economic development of the community and society at large. This is in addition to their primary missions of education (the first mission) and research (the second mission). One key aspect of this third mission is knowledge transfer, which includes setting up knowledge transfer centers and providing entrepreneurship education through active collaboration with external stakeholders, such as industries (Compagnucci and Spigarelli 2020). Supporting the entrepreneurial ideas of both university members and external entrepreneurs to bring innovations to market and society is a significant part of the third mission. Collaboration between public and academic libraries could foster regional growth driven by entrepreneurship and will also justify the investing of librarian efforts towards such initiatives.

As emphasized in the ALA Playbook and demonstrated by several public libraries supported through the ALA's Libraries Build Business initiative, even small libraries can successfully launch business support services. This can be achieved by strategically repositioning existing services to address the specific needs of local businesses. Importantly, limited funding does not have to be a barrier; libraries can leverage their current resources to tailor services for entrepreneurs and small enterprises. Innovation in business support can also emerge through collaborations with business support organizations, for instance practitioners, entrepreneurs. Indeed, partnerships are essential for initiating, growing, and scaling business support services within the library setting.

AI Adoption in Libraries: Factors Influencing Librarians and Entrepreneurs
The adoption of AI within libraries is contingent on multiple factors, with GenAI adoption comprising three stages, with each stage influenced by multiple factors. Many librarians remain hesitant to embrace AI due to knowledge gaps and concerns about data ethics and implementation challenges. Library managers must take a leadership role in fostering an AI-positive culture, ensuring that staff receive adequate training in AI literacy, prompt engineering, and ethical AI application. Additionally, they must foster experimentation culture driven by co-creation that leverages the adoption factors *that are common for both librarians and entrepreneurs* to identify number of use cases *(and misuse cases)* further strengthening curiosity and need based experimentations in libraries. A collaborative ecosystem can be established through interdisciplinary knowledge-sharing forums, AI experimentation spaces, and learning programs with joint involvement of librarians and the entrepreneurs. AI adoption should not be a static process, but a dynamic journey guided by structured experimentation. Need-based experimentation (NBE) should focus on AI solutions that address specific business challenges within library services, while curiosity-based experimentation (CBE) should encourage open-ended exploration of AI's potential benefits. Co-creation, involving both librarians and entrepreneurs in AI trials, will further strengthen adoption by ensuring that solutions are aligned with real-world business needs. Ethical considerations should also be embedded within AI adoption policies, ensuring that AI applications uphold data privacy regulations and align with the core mission of libraries as trusted knowledge centers.

Leveraging Co-Creation and Experimentation for AI Integration
AI integration in libraries must be an iterative process driven by continuous experimentation and co-creation. Libraries should establish dedicated AI experimentation labs, including the safe environment like GenAI sandboxes to explore the technology, where librarians and entrepreneurs collaborate on practical AI applications for business research and development. These labs can serve as incubators for testing AI-driven tools, measuring their effectiveness, and refining them for broader implementation. Library managers should also facilitate interdisciplinary collaborations, bringing together AI researchers, industry experts, and entrepreneurs to explore the potential of AI in library-driven business support services. A structured Monitoring & Evaluation (M&E) framework should be implemented to track AI adoption outcomes, ensuring that library-driven AI experiments are guided by data-driven insights. Successful AI applications should be documented and shared with the wider library community, encouraging peer learning and innovation diffusion. By fostering an experimentation-driven culture, libraries can become hubs

of AI-powered business intelligence, equipping entrepreneurs with the tools they need to make informed decisions.

Developing an AI Experimentation Policy for Libraries

Library AI adoption must be governed by clear policies that ensure ethical implementation, data security, and compliance with regulatory standards. Library managers should draft formal AI experimentation policies outlining the objectives, scope, and ethical considerations of AI-driven services. These policies should establish a framework for controlled AI trials, balancing innovation with risk management. Monitoring & Evaluation (M&E) should be integrated into AI experimentation, allowing library managers to assess the impact of AI applications in real time. Third party evaluators could be used to M&E framework, including the theory of change, indicators, survey questionaries etc. Library managers have to train the managers to conduct such M&E, foster their motivation to conduct it, and allocate the resources for it.

AI policies should also emphasize transparency, ensuring that entrepreneurs and patrons understand how AI is being used to enhance library business services. Furthermore, AI experimentation should follow a phased approach, starting with small-scale pilot projects before transitioning to broader implementations based on empirical success metrics. By adopting a structured policy approach, libraries can maximize the benefits of AI while mitigating potential risks. These experimentations as monitored & evaluated internally by the librarians should be treated as the way to improve further experimentations rather as the evaluation of the effectiveness. The evaluation of the effectiveness of the overall digital transformation program should be conducted *post-ant* by third party evaluators.

Identifying Practical AI Technologies for Entrepreneurial Support

Not all AI tools are equally suited for library business support services, making it essential for library managers to identify and integrate technologies that align with entrepreneurial needs. AI-driven research assistants such as ChatGPT, ASReview, and Connected Papers can streamline business research by automating literature reviews and trend analyses. Library managers should evaluate emerging AI tools through structured trials, ensuring that the technologies adopted are both user-friendly and aligned with the strategic objectives of business support services. By selecting AI tools that add tangible value to entrepreneurs, libraries can solidify their role as key enablers of innovation. There should not be limits on number of experimentations with number of AI technologies provided all experimentations aligns with the AI experimentation policy as adopted by the library. Future experimentations are driven by the experiences librarians gain through previous engagements with other AI technologies, often in collaboration with patrons.

Conclusion

10

This research provides a comprehensive exploration of the role of libraries in entrepreneurial support, particularly through the integration of artificial intelligence (AI) and emerging digital technologies. The study sheds light on the evolving business support roles of academic and public libraries, and the factors influencing AI adoption among librarians and entrepreneurs. It also introduces structured AI experimentation as a critical strategy for fostering innovation, ensuring ethical AI adoption, and enhancing business support services in libraries.

The findings highlight that Libraries, positioned as open innovation actors, can help entrepreneurs by curating business-relevant research, offering consultation services, and integrating AI-driven literature review tools. Additionally, structured AI experimentation, co-creation with entrepreneurs, and the implementation of monitoring and evaluation (M&E) frameworks emerge as essential components in optimizing AI adoption.

This book contributes to theory and practice by developing a novel AI adoption model tailored to the library context, experimentation-based approach using co-creation for AI adoption that could be need driven, curiosity driven or mix of both, proposing an AI experimentation policy framework, and identifying practical AI technologies that libraries can integrate into their services. The research underscores the importance of interdisciplinary collaboration, digital transformation, and ethical AI governance in enhancing the effectiveness of library-driven entrepreneurial support.

Ultimately, this study provides actionable insights for library managers, entrepreneurs, and policymakers, offering a roadmap for leveraging AI-driven innovations in business support services. Strengthening collaboration between libraries, entrepreneurs, and external innovation actors will be key to fostering sustainable, inclusive, and technology-enabled entrepreneurial ecosystems. Libraries must continue to evolve, embracing both

V. Gupta, *Libraries as Hubs for Entrepreneurship*, Synthesis Lectures on Information Concepts, Retrieval, and Services, https://doi.org/10.1007/978-3-032-03569-1_10

co-creation and structured experimentation- need-based and curiosity-driven, while developing dynamic capabilities that enable them to adapt, innovate, and optimize business support services in an ever-evolving technological landscape.

References

1. **Parker, K. R., Nitse, P. S., & Flowers, K. A. (2005).** Libraries as knowledge management centers. Library Management, 26(4/5), 176–189. https://doi.org/10.1108/01435120510596035
2. **Underwood, P. (2009).** Supporting the information needs of entrepreneurs in South Africa. *Library Review, 58*(8), 569–580. https://doi.org/10.1108/00242530910987064
3. **Hoppenfeld, J., Wyckoff, T., Henson, J. A. J., Mayotte, J. N., & Kirkwood, H. P. (2013).** Librarians and the Entrepreneurship Bootcamp for Veterans: Helping Disabled Veterans With Business Research. *Journal of Business & Finance Librarianship, 18*(4), 293–308. https://doi.org/10.1080/08963568.2013.825227
4. **Pryor, C. (2014).** Mind Your Business: Reaching the Small Business Owner and Entrepreneur Through Community Partnership and Programming. *Journal of Library Administration, 54*(3), 187–196. https://doi.org/10.1080/01930826.2014.915164
5. **Mort Feldmann, L. (2014).** Academic business librarians' assistance to community entrepreneurs. *Reference Services Review, 42*(1), 108–128. https://doi.org/10.1108/RSR-04-2013-0021
6. **Griffis, P. (2015).** Academic libraries as community resource partners for entrepreneurs. *Reference Services Review, 43*(3), 461–467. https://doi.org/10.1108/RSR-06-2015-0028
7. **Franks, J. E., & Johns, C. (2015).** Entrepreneur assistance & economic development in Florida libraries. *Reference Services Review, 43*(3), 400–418. https://doi.org/10.1108/RSR-03-2015-0014
8. **Mehra, B., Bishop, B., & Partee II, R. (2017).** How do public libraries assist small businesses in rural communities? An exploratory qualitative study in Tennessee. Libri, 67(4), 245–260. https://doi.org/10.1515/libri-2017-0042
9. **Faulkner, A. E. (2018).** Entrepreneurship resources in US public libraries: Website analysis. *Reference Services Review, 46*(1), 69–90. https://doi.org/10.1108/RSR-07-2017-0025
10. **Toane, C., & Figueiredo, R. (2018).** Toward core competencies for entrepreneurship librarians. Journal of Business & Finance Librarianship, 23(1), 35–62. https://doi.org/10.1080/08963568.2018.1448675
11. **Klotzbach-Russell, C., Rowley, E. M., & Starry, R. (2021).** Librarians in the LaunchPad: Building partnerships for entrepreneurial information literacy. *Journal of Business & Finance Librarianship, 27*(1), 41–56. https://doi.org/10.1080/08963568.2021.1982567
12. **Liu, G. (2021).** Exploring the information needs of student entrepreneurs: A meta-narrative synbook. *Journal of Business & Finance Librarianship, 26*(3–4), 254–290. https://doi.org/10.1080/08963568.2021.1955184
13. **Owolabi, K. A., Ugbala, C. P., Adeleke, A. O., Ovwas, D. E., & Akinbode, R. O. (2022).** Demographic Variables and Utilization of Public Library among Entrepreneurs in Nigeria. *The

V. Gupta, *Libraries as Hubs for Entrepreneurship*, Synthesis Lectures on Information Concepts, Retrieval, and Services, https://doi.org/10.1007/978-3-032-03569-1

International Information & Library Review, *55*(1), 44–55. https://doi.org/10.1080/10572317.2022.2070986

14. **Shehata, A. M. K., & Eldakar, M. A. M. (2023).** Fostering entrepreneurship in Omani academic libraries: Examining the present and pioneering future opportunities. *The Journal of Academic Librarianship*, *49*(5), 102763. https://doi.org/10.1016/j.acalib.2023.102763

15. **Bishop, B. W., Mehra, B., & Partee, R. P. (2016).** The role of rural public libraries in small business development. Public Library Quarterly, 35(1), 37–48. https://doi.org/10.1080/01616846.2016.1163971

16. **Cole, N., & Stenström, C. (2021).** The value of California's public libraries. Public Library Quarterly, 40(6), 481–503. https://doi.org/10.1080/01616846.2020.1816054

17. **Wynia Baluk, K., McQuire, S., Gillett, J., & Wyatt, D. (2020).** Aging in a Digital Society: Exploring How Canadian and Australian Public Library Systems Program for Older Adults. Public Library Quarterly, 40(6), 521–539. https://doi.org/10.1080/01616846.2020.1811612

18. **Stanikūnienė, B., Kvedaraitė, N., & Žvirelienė, R. (2024).** Innovative solutions of public libraries offered to business. Journal of Librarianship and Information Science, 56(4), 884-895. https://doi.org/10.1177/09610006231178569

19. **Scott, R. (2011).** The role of public libraries in community building. Public Library Quarterly, 30(3), 191-227, https://doi.org/10.1080/01616846.2011.599283.

20. **Lo, L. S. (2024a).** Transforming academic librarianship through AI reskilling: Insights from the GPT-4 exploration program. The Journal of Academic Librarianship, 50(3). https://doi.org/10.1016/j.acalib.2024.102883

21. **Farney T. (2021).** Tabatha. Library technology: Innovating technologies, services, and practices. College & Undergraduate Libraries, 27(2–4), 51–55. https://doi.org/10.1080/10691316.2020.1952776

22. **Ippoliti C., Kiersten M., & Shea S. (2021).** Make labs, not war: Rethinking library creative technology services through a critical making lens. College & Undergraduate Libraries, 27(2-4), 354-368. https://doi.org/10.1080/10691316.2021.1908199

23. **Khan, A.U., Rafi, M., Zhang, Z. and Khan, A. (2023).** Determining the impact of technological modernization and management capabilities on user satisfaction and trust in library services. Global Knowledge, Memory and Communication, Vol. 72 No. 6/7, pp. 593-611. https://doi.org/10.1108/GKMC-06-2021-0095

24. **Chu, S.K.W. & Du, H.S. (2012).** Social networking tools for academic libraries. Journal of Librarianship and Information Science, 45(1), 64-75, https://doi.org/10.1177/0961000611434361

25. **Chen, X. (2023).** ChatGPT and its possible impact on library reference services. Internet Reference Services Quarterly, 27(2), 121–129. https://doi.org/10.1080/10875301.2023.2181262

26. **Cox, C., & Tzoc, E. (2023).** ChatGPT: Implications for academic libraries. College & Research Libraries News, 84(3), 99, https://doi.org/10.5860/crln.84.3.99

27. **Kannegiser, S. (2022).** Creating an augmented reality orientation using learning and design theories. College & undergraduate libraries, 28(2), 148-164. https://doi.org/10.1080/10691316.2021.1896980

28. **Winkler B. & Kiszl P. (2022).** Views of Academic Library Directors on Artificial Intelligence: A Representative Survey in Hungary. New Review of Academic Librarianship, 28:3, 256-278, https://doi.org/10.1080/13614533.2021.1930076

29. **Hervieux, S. and Wheatley, A. (2021).** Perceptions of artificial intelligence: A survey of academic librarians in Canada and the United States. The Journal of Academic Librarianship, 47(1), p.102270, https://doi.org/10.1016/j.acalib.2020.102270

30. **Yoon, J., Andrews, J. E., & Ward, H. L. (2022).** Perceptions on adopting artificial intelligence and related technologies in libraries: Public and academic librarians in North America. *Library Hi Tech, 40*(6), 1893-1915. https://doi.org/10.1108/LHT-07-2021-0229

31. **Lo, L. S. (2024b).** Evaluating AI literacy in academic libraries: A survey study with a focus on US employees. College & Research Libraries, 85(5), 635-S668. https://doi.org/10.5860/crl.85.5.635

32. **Kaushal, V., & Yadav, R. (2022).** The role of chatbots in academic libraries: An experience-based perspective. *Journal of the Australian Library and Information Association, 71*(3), 215-232. https://doi.org/10.1080/24750158.2022.2106403

33. **Echedom A.U. & Okuonghae O. (2021).** Transforming academic library operations in Africa with artificial intelligence: Opportunities and challenges: A review paper. New Review of Academic Librarianship, 27:2, 243-255, https://doi.org/10.1080/13614533.2021.1906715

34. **Ajani Y.A, Tella A., Yetunde Salawu K.Y & Abdullahi F. (2022).** Perspectives of Librarians on Awareness and Readiness of Academic Libraries to Integrate Artificial Intelligence for Library Operations and Services in Nigeria. Internet Reference Services Quarterly, 26:4, 213-230, https://doi.org/10.1080/10875301.2022.2086196

35. **Brzustowicz, R. (2023).** From ChatGPT to CatGPT: The Implications of Artificial Intelligence on Library Cataloging. Information Technology and Libraries, 42(3). https://doi.org/10.5860/ital.v42i3.16295

36. **Johnson, S., Owens, E., Menendez, H., & Kim, D. (2024).** Using ChatGPT-generated essays in library instruction. The Journal of Academic Librarianship, 50(2), 102863. https://doi.org/10.1016/j.acalib.2024.102863

37. **Adetayo, A.J. (2023).** Artificial intelligence chatbots in academic libraries: the rise of ChatGPT. Library Hi Tech News, Vol. 40 No. 3, pp. 18-21. https://doi.org/10.1108/LHTN-01-2023-0007

38. **Lund, B. D., & Wang, T. (2023).** Chatting about ChatGPT: How may AI and GPT impact academia and libraries?. Library Hi Tech News, 40(3), 26–29. https://doi.org/10.1108/LHTN-01-2023-0009

39. **Lappalainen Y., & Narayanan N. (2023).** Aisha: A Custom AI Library Chatbot Using the ChatGPT API. Journal of Web Librarianship. https://doi.org/10.1080/19322909.2023.2221477

40. **Yang, S. Q., & Mason, S. (2024).** Beyond the Algorithm: Understanding How ChatGPT Handles Complex Library Queries. Internet Reference Services Quarterly, 28(2), 97-151. https://doi.org/10.1080/10875301.2023.2291441

41. **Marshall, D., & DuBose, J. (2024).** AI in academic libraries: The future is now. Public Services Quarterly, 20(2), 150-155. https://doi.org/10.1080/15228959.2024.2331124

42. **Formanek, M. (2024).** Exploring the potential of large language models and generative artificial intelligence (GPT): Applications in Library and Information Science. Journal of Librarianship and Information Science, 0(0). https://doi.org/10.1177/09610006241241066

43. **Torres, J. M. (2024).** Leveraging ChatGPT and bard for academic librarians and information professionals: a case study of developing pedagogical strategies using generative AI models. Journal of Business & Finance Librarianship, 1-14. https://doi.org/10.1080/08963568.2024.2321729

44. **Lund, B. D., Khan, D., & Yuvaraj, M. (2024).** ChatGPT in medical libraries, possibilities and future directions: An integrative review. Health Information & Libraries Journal, 41:04–15, Wiley. https://doi.org/10.1111/hir.12518

45. **Fui-Hoon Nah, F., Zheng, R., Cai, J., Siau, K., & Chen, L. (2023).** Generative AI and ChatGPT: Applications, challenges, and AI-human collaboration. Journal of Information Technology Case and Application Research, 25(3), 277–304. https://doi.org/10.1080/15228053.2023.2233814

46. **Panda, S. K., Bhatt, A., & Satapathy, A. (2024).** ChatGPT and its role in academic libraries: A discussion. *New Review of Academic Librarianship*, 1–15. https://doi.org/10.1080/13614533. 2024.2381510

47. **Nehra, S. S., & Bansode, S. Y. (2024).** Exploring the prospects and perils of integrating artificial intelligence and ChatGPT in academic and research libraries (ARL): Challenges and opportunity. *Journal of Web Librarianship*, 1–22. https://doi.org/10.1080/19322909.2024.239 0413

48. **Sanchez-Ramos, Luis, Lifeng Lin, and Roberto Romero. (2023).** Beware of references when using ChatGPT as a source of information to write scientific articles. American Journal of Obstetrics & Gynecology. https://doi.org/10.1016/j.ajog.2023.04.004

49. **Elali, Faisal R., and Leena N. Rachid. (2023).** AI-generated research paper fabrication and plagiarism in the scientific community. Patterns, 4(3). https://doi.org/10.1016/j.patter.2023. 100706

50. **Day, Terence. (2023).** A preliminary investigation of fake peer-reviewed citations and references generated by ChatGPT. The Professional Geographer, 1-4. https://doi.org/10.1080/003 30124.2023.2190373

51. **Ray, Partha Pratim. (2023).** ChatGPT: A comprehensive review on background, applications, key challenges, bias, ethics, limitations and future scope. Internet of Things and Cyber-Physical Systems, 3: 121-154. https://doi.org/10.1016/j.iotcps.2023.04.003

52. **Gravel, Jocelyn, Madeleine D'Amours-Gravel, and Esli Osmanlliu. (2023).** Learning to fake it: Limited responses and fabricated references provided by ChatGPT for medical questions. Mayo Clinic Proceedings: Digital Health, 1(3): 226-234. https://doi.org/10.1016/j.mcp dig.2023.05.004

53. **Huang, Y. H. (2024).** Exploring the implementation of artificial intelligence applications among academic libraries in Taiwan. *Library Hi Tech, 42*(3), 885-905. https://doi.org/10.1108/ LHT-03-2022-0159

54. **Lo, L. S. (2023).** AI policies across the globe: Implications and recommendations for libraries. IFLA Journal, 49(4), 645-649. https://doi.org/10.1177/03400352231196172

55. **Bradley, F. (2022).** Representation of Libraries in Artificial Intelligence Regulations and Implications for Ethics and Practice. Journal of the Australian Library and Information Association, 71(3), 189–200. https://doi.org/10.1080/24750158.2022.2101911

56. **Liu, Y.D., Sun, J., Zhang, Z.J., Wu, M., Sima, H. and Ooi, Y.M. (2024).** How AI impacts companies' dynamic capabilities: Lessons from six Chinese construction firms. *Research-Technology Management*, Vol. 67 No. 3, pp. 64–76. https://doi.org/10.1080/08956308.2024. 2324407

57. **Akakpo, M. G. (2024).** Skilled for the future: Information literacy for AI use by university students in Africa and the role of librarians. Internet Reference Services Quarterly, 28(1), 19–26. https://doi.org/10.1080/10875301.2023.2280566

58. **Fruehauf, E., Beman-Cavallaro, A., & Schmidt, L. (2024).** Developing a foundation for the informational needs of generative AI users through the means of established interdisciplinary relationships. *The Journal of Academic Librarianship, 50*(3), 102876. https://doi.org/10.1016/ j.acalib.2024.102876

59. **Bridges, L. M., McElroy, K., & Welhouse, Z. (2024).** Generative artificial intelligence: 8 critical questions for libraries. Journal of Library Administration, 64(1), 66–79. https://doi.org/ 10.1080/01930826.2024.2292484

60. **Frow, P., Nenonen, S., Payne, A., & Storbacka, K.** (2015). Managing co-creation design: A strategic approach to innovation. *British Journal of Management, 26*(3), 463–483. https://doi. org/10.1111/1467-8551.12087

61. **Piller, F., Ihl, C., & Vossen, A.** (2011). Customer co-creation: Open innovation with customers. In V. Wittke & H. Hanekop (Eds.), *New forms of collaboration and innovation on the Internet* (pp. 31–63). Universitätsverlag Göttingen.

62. **Yang, Y., Luo, J., & Lan, T.** (2022). An empirical assessment of a modified artificially intelligent device use acceptance model—From the task-oriented perspective. *Frontiers in Psychology, 13*, 4900. https://doi.org/10.3389/fpsyg.2022.975307

63. **Gursoy, D., Chi, O. H., Lu, L., & Nunkoo, R.** (2019). Consumers' acceptance of artificially intelligent device use in service delivery. *International Journal of Information Management, 49*, 157–169. https://doi.org/10.1016/j.ijinfomgt.2019.03.008

64. **Kelly, S., Kaye, S. A., & Oviedo-Trespalacios, O.** (2022). What factors contribute to acceptance of artificial intelligence? A systematic review. *Telematics and Informatics, 68*, 101925. https://doi.org/10.1016/j.tele.2022.101925

65. **Weiss, C. H.** (1995). Nothing as practical as good theory: Exploring theory-based evaluation for comprehensive community initiatives for children and families. In J. Connell, A. Kubisch, L. Schorr, & C. Weiss (Eds.), New approaches to evaluating comprehensive community initiatives (pp. 65–92). The Aspen Institute.

66. **Sullivan, H., & Stewart, M.** (2006). Who owns the theory of change? Evaluation, 12(2), 179–199. https://doi.org/10.1177/1356389006066971

67. **Breuer, E., Lee, L., De Silva, M. & Lund C.** (2015). Using theory of change to design and evaluate public health interventions: a systematic review. Implementation Sci 11, 63 (2015). https://doi.org/10.1186/s13012-016-0422-6.

68. **Savaya, R., & Waysman, M.** (2005). The Logic Model: A Tool for Incorporating Theory in Development and Evaluation of Programs. Administration in Social Work, 29(2), 85–103. https://doi.org/10.1300/J147v29n02_06.

69. **Bucher, J. A.** (2010). Using the logic model for planning and evaluation: examples for new users. Home Health Care Management & Practice, 22(5), 325-333. https://doi.org/10.1177/108 4822309353154.

70. **Urquhart, C.** (2018). Principles and practice in impact assessment for academic libraries. Information and Learning Science, 119(1/2), 121-134. https://doi.org/10.1108/ILS-06-2017-0053

71. **Yim, M., Fellows, M., & Coward, C.** (2020). Mixed-methods library evaluation integrating the patron, library, and external perspectives: The case of Namibia regional libraries. Evaluation and Program Planning, 79, 101782. https://doi.org/10.1016/j.evalprogplan.2020.101782

72. **Poll, R., & Payne, P.** (2006). Impact measures for libraries and information services. Library Hi Tech, 24(4), 547-562. https://doi.org/10.1108/07378830610715419

73. **Aregbesola, A., Owolabi, S. E., & Adebisi, T.** (2024). Going to the cities: The strategic roles of public libraries in promoting sustainable development goals. Public Library Quarterly, 43(3), 367-384. https://doi.org/10.1080/01616846.2023.2253692

74. **American Library Association.** (2023). Libraries build business. Retrieved August 1, 2024, from https://alair.ala.org/server/api/core/bitstreams/2e276162-edb2-4fbc-9d2b-26ba8e b43691/content

75. **Dunn, A.** (2021). Monitoring and Evaluation of Public Libraries: A Case of Public Libraries in Namibia, 322–327.

76. **Matthews, J. R.** (2017). The evaluation and measurement of library services (2nd ed., 480 Pages). Bloomsbury Publishing USA. https://doi.org/10.5040/9798400648236

77. **Saunders, L.** (2015). Academic libraries' strategic plans: Top trends and under-recognized areas. *The Journal of Academic Librarianship, 41*(3), 285–291. https://doi.org/10.1016/j.aca lib.2015.03.011

78. **Okunlaya, R. O., Syed Abdullah, N., & Alias, R. A.** (2022). Artificial intelligence (AI) library services: Innovative conceptual framework for the digital transformation of university education. *Library Hi Tech, 40*(6), 1869–1892. https://doi.org/10.1108/LHT-07-2021-0242

79. **Hamad, F., Tbaishat, D., & Al-Fadel, M.** (2017). The role of social networks in enhancing the library profession and promoting academic library services: A comparative study of the University of Jordan and Al-Balqaa' Applied University. Journal of Librarianship and Information Science, 49(4), 397–408. https://doi.org/10.1177/0961000616656043

80. **Semode, F. D., Ejitagha, S., & Baro, E. E.** (2017). Social networking sites: Changing roles, skills, and use by librarians in tertiary institutions in Nigeria. Library Philosophy and Practice (e-journal). http://digitalcommons.unl.edu/libphilprac/1500

81. **Lu, L., Cai, R., & Gursoy, D.** (2019). Developing and validating a service robot integration willingness scale. International Journal of Hospitality Management, 80, 36–51. https://doi.org/10.1016/j.ijhm.2019.01.005

82. **Romero Rodríguez, J. M., Ramírez-Montoya, M. S., Buenestado Fernández, M., & Lara Lara, F.** (2023). Use of ChatGPT at university as a tool for complex thinking: Students' perceived usefulness. Cultura de los Cuidados, 12(2), 323–339. https://doi.org/10.7821/naer.2023.7.145

83. **Emon, M. M. H., Hassan, F., Nahid, M. H., & Rattanawiboonsom, V.** (2023). Predicting adoption intention of artificial intelligence. AIUB Journal of Science and Engineering (AJSE, 22(2), 189–199. https://doi.org/10.53799/AJSE.V22I2.797

84. **Khan, A.** (2020). Investigating the factors influencing librarians' intention toward the adoption of Koha—An open-source integrated library system in Pakistan. Library Philosophy and Practice (e-journal), (4360), 1–52. https://digitalcommons.unl.edu/libphilprac/4360

85. **Gupta, V., Gupta, C., Swacha, J., & Rubalcaba, L.** (2022). Prototyping technology adoption among entrepreneurship and innovation libraries for rural health innovations. Library Hi Tech, 42(6), 1760–1795. https://doi.org/10.1108/LHT-03-2023-0120

86. **Frederick, D. E.** (2024). Prompt engineering – a disruption in information seeking? Library Hi Tech News, 41(3), 1–5. https://doi.org/10.1108/LHTN-03-2024-0037

87. **Duong, C. D., Vu, T. N., & Ngo, T. V. N.** (2023). Applying a modified technology acceptance model to explain higher education students' usage of ChatGPT: A serial multiple mediation model with knowledge sharing as a moderator. The International Journal of Management Education, 21(3), 100883. https://doi.org/10.1016/j.ijme.2023.100883

88. **Strzelecki, A.** (2023). To use or not to use ChatGPT in higher education? A study of students' acceptance and use of technology. Interactive Learning Environments, 1–14. https://doi.org/10.1080/10494820.2023.2209881

89. **Mustafa, S., & Wen, Z.** (2022). How to achieve maximum participation of users in technical versus non-technical online Q&A communities? International Journal of Electronic Commerce, 26(1), 1–25. https://doi.org/10.1080/10864415.2022.2123645

90. **Jo, H., & Bang, Y.** (2023). Analyzing ChatGPT adoption drivers with the TOEK framework. Scientific Reports, 13, 22606. https://doi.org/10.1038/s41598-023-49710-0

91. **Compagnucci, L., & Spigarelli, F.** (2020). The third mission of the university: A systematic literature review on potentials and constraints. Technological Forecasting and Social Change, 161, 120284. https://doi.org/10.1016/j.techfore.2020.120284

92. **Gupta, V., & Rubalcaba, L.** (2021). University libraries as open innovation partners: Harnessing hidden potential to foster global entrepreneurship. The Journal of Academic Librarianship, 48(2), 102432. https://doi.org/10.1016/j.acalib.2021.102432

93. **Gupta, V., Rubalcaba, L., Gupta, C., & Pereira, L.** (2022). Library social networking sites for fostering startup business globalization through strategic partnerships. The Journal of Academic Librarianship, 48(6), 102504. https://doi.org/10.1016/j.acalib.2022.102504

94. **Gupta, V. (2023a).** Mobile Application Development Lab and University of Toronto Libraries: Advancing innovation through synergistic collaboration. Internet Reference Services Quarterly, 27(4), 223–231. https://doi.org/10.1080/10875301.2023.2282931

95. **Gupta, V. (2025a).** Factors influencing librarian adoptions of ChatGPT technology for entrepreneurial support. Library Hi Tech, ahead-of-print. https://doi.org/10.1108/LHT-09-2024-0463

96. **Gupta, V. (2024a).** Factors influencing librarian adoption of ChatGPT technology for entrepreneurial support: A study protocol. Journal of Economy and Technology, 2, 166–173. https://doi.org/10.1016/j.ject.2024.04.006

97. **Gupta, V. (2024b).** An empirical evaluation of a generative artificial intelligence technology adoption model from entrepreneurs' perspectives. Systems, 12(3), 103. https://doi.org/10.3390/systems12030103

98. **Gupta, V., & Yang, H. (2024a).** Generative artificial intelligence (AI) technology adoption model for entrepreneurs: Case of ChatGPT. Internet Reference Services Quarterly, 28(2), 223–242. https://doi.org/10.1080/10875301.2023.2300114

99. **Gupta, V., & Yang, H. (2024b).** Study protocol for factors influencing the adoption of ChatGPT technology by startups: Perceptions and attitudes of entrepreneurs. PLOS ONE, 19(2). https://doi.org/10.1371/journal.pone.0298427

100. **Gupta, V. (2024c).** From hype to strategy: Navigating the reality of experimental strategic adoption of AI technologies in libraries. Reference Services Review, ahead-of-print. https://doi.org/10.1108/RSR-08-2024-0042

101. **Gupta, V., & Gupta, C. (2023a).** Leveraging AI technologies in libraries through experimentation-driven frameworks. Internet Reference Services Quarterly, 27(4), 211–222. https://doi.org/10.1080/10875301.2023.2240773

102. **Gupta, V., & Gupta, C. (2023b).** Synchronizing innovation: Unveiling the synergy of need-based and curiosity-based experimentation in AI technology adoption for libraries. Library Hi Tech News, 40(9), 15–17. https://doi.org/10.1108/LHTN-07-2023-0127

103. **Gupta, V., & Gupta, C. (2023c).** Experimentation-driven frameworks for AI technology adoption in libraries: Practical implementation in library. College & Undergraduate Libraries, 30(3), 95–103. https://doi.org/10.1080/10691316.2023.2266819

104. **Gupta, V. (2024d).** Innovating library services: Co-creation, experimentation, and enhanced business value tool for technological advancements. Public Library Quarterly, 44(1), 74–90. https://doi.org/10.1080/01616846.2024.2364522

105. **Gupta, V. (2023b).** Navigating innovation: An enhanced business value calculator and its impact on library service innovations for entrepreneurs and businesses. *Internet Reference Services Quarterly, 28*(1), 27–37. https://doi.org/10.1080/10875301.2023.2289418

106. **Gupta, V. (2024e).** AI experimentation policy for libraries: Balancing innovation and data privacy. Public Library Quarterly, 1–21. https://doi.org/10.1080/01616846.2024.2445356

107. **Gupta, V. (2024f).** From experimentation to insight: Structured reporting of AI experimentations in libraries. Journal of Web Librarianship, 1–12. https://doi.org/10.1080/19322909.2025.2450539

108. **Gupta, V. (2024g).** Boosting entrepreneurial support in libraries: Introducing ASReview for reference librarians. Journal of Web Librarianship, 18(4), 233–240. https://doi.org/10.1080/19322909.2024.2428859

109. **Gupta, V., & Gupta, C. (2023d).** Transforming entrepreneurial research: Leveraging library research services and technology innovations for rapid information discovery. Online Information Review, 48(3), 491–499. https://doi.org/10.1108/OIR-04-2023-0156

110. **Gupta, V. (2023c).** Citation Gecko technology for research and entrepreneurship. Library Hi Tech News, ahead-of-print. https://doi.org/10.1108/LHTN-04-2023-0060

111. **Kim, D., Kumar, V., & Kumar, U. (2010).** Performance assessment framework for supply chain partnership. Supply Chain Management, 15(3), 187–195. https://doi.org/10.1108/13598541011039947

112. **Gupta, V. (2025b).** Evaluating library entrepreneurial services impact: Introducing project outcome as an evaluation tool. Public Services Quarterly, 21(2), 109–126. https://doi.org/10.1080/15228959.2025.2467718

113. **American Library Association. (2022).** Libraries Build Business Playbook. Online accessed on 01st August 2024. Available at: https://www.ala.org/sites/default/files/advocacy/content/Workforce/LBB_Playbook_web_020222.pdf

114. **American Library Association. (2023).** Libraries Build Business Initiative – Final M&E Report. Online accessed on 01st August 2024. Available at: https://www.ala.org/sites/default/files/advocacy/content/Workforce/LBB%20Evaluation%20-%20Final%20Report%202022-01-27.pdf.

MIX
Papier aus verantwortungsvollen Quellen
Paper from responsible sources
FSC® C105338

If you have any concerns about our products,
you can contact us on
ProductSafety@springernature.com

In case Publisher is established outside the EU,
the EU authorized representative is:
Springer Nature Customer Service Center GmbH
Europaplatz 3, 69115 Heidelberg, Germany

Printed by Libri Plureos GmbH
in Hamburg, Germany